BLUNT FORCE YOGA

TRUE CRIME MEMOIR

BY LISA JONES

Published by Verbal Construction, LLC
Denver, Colorado, USA
book@yogadeath.com

DEDICATION

For Quinn and Belle

ACKNOWLEDGMENTS

Thanks to Kit Brown-Hoekstra, Paula Kurtz, and Meghan S. Morris for keeping me concise and on point.
Thanks to everyone I've ever talked to about Dana's case. Your thoughts have helped to shape this book.
Thanks to Steve and Laura, Neil and Elaine, aunts, uncles, cousins, friends, and Camerados.
Thanks to you for reading this.

1. Take the Notebook

"We don't blame the police," my brother Stephen said. He interrupted me because I was criticizing detectives for their indifference about our sister's suspicious death. Stephen saw no use in my insulting Bryan, the detective who was listening to our meeting on speakerphone.

"No, we don't blame the police," I agreed grudgingly. Police had botched the investigation, I believed, but they weren't responsible for Dana's death.

We were in a glass tower conference room at Fifth and Flower in downtown Los Angeles with a panoramic view toward Pasadena. It was late afternoon on August 24, 2015. Dana had been dead for a year and a half. She had been murdered by her husband Huck, we believed, in March 2014. So far, Huck had gotten away with it.

We had asked the Long Beach police to explain why they believed Dana's death was a catastrophic "yoga accident" in which a blunt-force blow had cracked her skull, rendering her almost immediately brain-dead. Women murdered by their husbands or boyfriends are commonplace. Yoga fatalities from head trauma are so rare they're nonexistent. What were detectives thinking?

The lead detective was a glib, perspiring man named Todd Johnson. He pointed to Huck's statements, many of them demonstrable lies, as "proof" of Huck's innocence in the matter.

For instance, Huck claimed that one year prior to Dana's death, during a visit to Hawaii, Dana had fallen while doing yoga and hit her head. She had consulted a doctor who said Dana was fine. Johnson accepted this as true, even though Dana had not visited Hawaii in years. If she had sought medical care, there would have been a record, such as a payment or an insurance claim. Johnson didn't ask Huck to provide evidence of this purported medical visit. Rather, Johnson took Huck's word for it

1

that an alleged, nonfatal "yoga fall" was a logical prelude to a deadly yoga accident.

My parents, brother, and I couldn't understand why Johnson declined to fact-check Huck. Our Denver-based lawyers advised us to hire an attorney in Los Angeles to find out why Dana's case had been closed, and to persuade police to reopen the investigation.

In February 2015, we hired Carmen Trutanich, a robust personality accustomed to seeing his name in the news. His nickname was Nuch, rhymes with smooch. He had once been elected Los Angeles City Attorney. We wanted someone who could speak to powerful people on our behalf, and Nuch knew everyone.

In Nuch's conference room at our August 2015 meeting, Nuch sat at one end of a long table with his paralegal Stacey Sautter and a private investigator named Randy Candias. My brother and I sat at the other end, across the table from Curt Livesay. Curt seemed more like a polite professor emeritus than a hard-boiled prosecutor. He had once been chief deputy district attorney in Los Angeles. He was the one who decided to seek the death penalty in the infamous cases of serial killers Richard "The Night Stalker" Ramirez and William Bonin, known as the "Freeway Killer."

On the table between Curt and me was the speakerphone that carried Bryan's voice. Bryan McMahon was a semi-retired homicide detective in Long Beach who, back in the day, had trained Detective Johnson.

I met Bryan in person only once, at a marathon meeting in another of Nuch's impressive conference rooms, in March 2015. My first impression was that he resembled Dana's husband Huck. He had a similar, graying Van Dyke mustache and beard.

Bryan said he had analyzed more than 15 hours of video recordings related to the case. He billed us for the mere six hours he'd spent on the task. Maybe he was doing us a favor, billing us for less time than the job logically would take. Still, it told me that something about Bryan didn't add up.

Despite the presence of 12 surveillance cameras in Dana's house, none were in the yoga room, and none were in the hallway leading to the yoga room. In fact, most of the house was camera-free. Even so, Bryan asserted that the surveillance system gave a clear picture of what had happened to Dana.

Bryan expressed certainties that, to me, were ridiculous. For instance, the lower back of Dana's scalp was split by a laceration that was almost two inches long. Strangely, the wound wasn't bleeding when paramedics arrived. How did police explain the lack of blood at the scene?

Bryan was confident that the concrete floor under Dana's head applied pressure and prevented bleeding. To me, this made no sense because of the curve of her skull. Wouldn't it be like a cracked sphere full of liquid, leaking? A flat floor couldn't apply compression evenly across the entire breadth of a curved, two-inch rupture, could it? Bryan was certain that it could and did.

Bryan implied that, regardless of what I knew about Dana and Huck, it was just my opinion, mere hearsay at best, and therefore of no value. His opinions and those of Detective Johnson were facts because they were arrived at objectively. I couldn't possibly be objective, so I couldn't analyze facts. I had to take Bryan's word for it that he knew better than me.

For the record, in telling Dana's story, I'm expressing my own opinions and impressions informed by my own experiences and observations, plus hearsay regarding the opinions and observations of others, as well as provable facts. I'm including verbatim quotes from police reports and other documents. I'm not claiming objectivity. I doubt genuine objectivity is achievable by anyone ever.

That said, I had a gut feeling Bryan was trying to misdirect or thwart the investigation somehow. At the time, I couldn't fathom why he would. Bryan was revered by people in Long Beach as a god of murder investigation. He had been named "Investigator of the Year" by the California Homicide Investigators Association. When I asked Stacey if she felt something "off" about Bryan, she vouched for his integrity.

Was my gut feeling simply wrong, or did Bryan have a conflict of interest? He spoke as if he had been involved with Dana's case prior to being hired by Nuch on our behalf. According to public records, Long Beach police paid Bryan $19,038 for investigative work in 2014, the year of Dana's death. Was Bryan's professional loyalty with us as his client, or with the Long Beach Police Department (LBPD)? Was he seeking answers about Dana's case, or was he protecting his one-time trainee Detective Johnson? It didn't occur to me that Bryan might be covering up a welter of lapses and lies in the LBPD.

If Nuch recognized a conflict of interest regarding Bryan, he never mentioned it to me. It didn't occur to me that Nuch, too, might be conflicted due to his long-standing loyalties to police and powers-that-be. I thought we were all on the same side, all wanting clarity about the facts, all wanting wrongs to be put right.

By August 2015, more than six months had passed since my in-person meeting with Bryan. In the interim, my dad had paid Nuch and his associates close to $100,000 in retainers and hourly fees. My dad was willing to pay whatever price to kick over rocks in pursuit of justice for Dana.

Rocks were kicked, and Nuch's team shrugged their shoulders. Yes, many facts in Dana's case indicated that, more likely than not, she was murdered. But Bryan was sure it was just a terrible yoga accident. Therefore, nothing could be done. Our only option was to keep the team on retainer until somehow, something changed.

It seemed to my brother Stephen that our desire for justice was being exploited. For example, my dad was billed more than $20,000 by Nuch's office for the drafting of a wrongful death complaint against Huck. We were never allowed to see the draft, and Nuch never filed the complaint in court. What was the point of the expense?

To us, Dana's death was a criminal matter that should be dealt with by a law enforcement agency. "If they don't see it was murder, they'll never see," Stephen said to me. It was obvious to us that Detective Johnson had made up his mind very early in the case. He didn't welcome new information. What was the point, then, of employing lawyers and investigators to hunt for fresh clues? The investigation was an unsustainable expenditure of dad's finite resources, and it was going nowhere. Therefore, Stephen and I traveled to L.A. in August 2015 to fire Nuch.

Firing Nuch was difficult because he continued to offer fresh hope. For instance, he said he could obtain audio recordings made by the medical examiner during Dana's autopsy. Stephen and I perked up, hopeful about finding new clues. Bryan immediately countered, saying medical examiners don't make audio recordings. Asking the coroner's office for help was no use.

This was how meetings went. Nuch suggested new avenues of investigation; Bryan quickly blocked them. Was Nuch fighting to get answers, or not? We weren't sure.

Also, there was the notebook. Detective Johnson had given Bryan pages and pages of police reports, plus 188 digital photos taken by police, and 15 hours of surveillance video recordings seized from Dana and Huck's house. Nuch's office made copies, put the digital evidence on compact disc, and packaged it all in a three-ring binder. I'd guess a dozen copies of the notebook were floating around.

In March 2015, I was given the notebook at my in-person meeting with Bryan. After hours of answering his questions about Dana, I was asked to leave the meeting so Bryan could confer with other investigators, namely Stacey, Randy, retired Long Beach Police Officer Valerie (Rose) Romero, and retired Los Angeles Police Officer Tyler Izen.

Bryan said I could take the notebook, share it with my family, and get back to him with questions.

I sat down with the notebook on the first bench I saw, in the courtyard in front of Nuch's building. As I read police reports, I searched for something to help me see why they exonerated Huck. I couldn't find it. Instead, the reports made it clear to me that Huck had killed Dana and lied about it. Why were police so gullible?

I planned to make copies for my parents and Stephen. First, I made a quick trip across the street to my hotel room at The Standard. My phone buzzed with a call from Stacey. She asked me to return the notebook as soon as possible.

I walked back to Nuch's office. The conference room was empty except for Stacey and me. She looked weary, as if she'd been in a fierce argument. "There's been a development," she said. It would be bad for me if the notebook were found in my possession, she said. I couldn't guess how it could be bad for me, or who might be examining my possessions. I gave her the notebook.

I soon regretted parting with it. Bryan insisted the surveillance video from my sister's house cleared Huck of all suspicion. I had seen only the brief, silent clip that Bryan had shown me.

In the clip, Dana's dog Enzo sat on a sofa down the hall from the "yoga room." At a specific moment, the dog appeared to startle because of a sound that seemingly came from the direction of the yoga room. Enzo remained on the sofa, looking perplexed. Next, Huck entered the scene, coming from the direction of the yoga room. Huck faced the camera and acted as if he was brushing his teeth. He walked off camera toward the yoga room. Minutes later, Huck called 911.

According to Bryan, this clip proved that Dana had fallen and hit her head while doing yoga, making a sound that startled the dog. Plus, Huck had called 911 before Dana was dead. To Bryan, this proved Huck's innocence.

To me, it proved that Huck had fooled Bryan. If I'd kept the notebook and the video it contained, I might have been able to show Bryan how and why he had been misled. I assumed that, after firing Nuch, I'd never have a chance.

Perhaps Nuch's team had done all they could for us, in good faith, and knew there was no reason to continue the investigation. I figured I had nothing to lose by arguing with Bryan, and with all of them. I recounted my reasons for believing Dana was murdered. Why couldn't they see? Why didn't they care?

Bryan, on speakerphone, was audibly exasperated with me. He said I needed to accept the hard truth that Dana had died in a freak yoga accident.

Bryan brought up a completely different case, one that, like Dana's, had been ruled an accident by the L.A. County Coroner's Office. After the meeting, I obtained a copy of the autopsy report from that case because media stories about it sounded implausible.

According to the medical examiner, R&B singer Charmayne Maxwell, at her multimillion-dollar house above Sunset Boulevard in West Hollywood, had been stabbed once in the left side of her neck, and once in her upper chest. Each stab wound was more than two inches deep, penetrating in a downward direction. Her left jugular vein had been completely cut. Her live-in boyfriend said he found her supine in a pool of blood and tried to give her CPR for 10 to 20 minutes before paramedics arrived. She bled to death due to sharp force injury. The report noted that there was blood on the soles of her feet, somehow.

Despite the stab wounds and other injuries on the woman's body, such as bruises and chipped front teeth, Los Angeles Police Homicide Detective David Vinton said there were no signs of foul play. The medical examiner concluded that Maxwell had died accidentally. Media reports embellished this conclusion, claiming she had fallen on the stem of a broken wine glass.

These things happen, Bryan asserted. Why, then, was it so hard for me to believe Dana had died from yoga? The video clip proved it.

Stephen had never seen the video. Nuch projected it onto a screen. We watched the clip Bryan had shown me months earlier, plus a few minutes more.

"He's acting so suspiciously," Stephen said. "Look."

Stephen was right. Huck's behavior was odd. Paramedics wheeled Dana out of the house on a gurney. Huck stood at the front gate, held up his phone, and took a photo of her as she was being put into the ambulance. After she was taken away, he paced histrionically in front of surveillance cameras as he made several phone calls. One of the calls he made was to my mother. Huck told my mom that Dana had injured herself severely while doing yoga.

Paramedics told police they didn't know what was wrong with Dana at the scene. Had she fainted or suffered a stroke? They didn't know. Why would Huck presume to know what was wrong before emergency-room doctors even had a chance to evaluate her?

After the ambulance left, video shows that Huck remained at the house for another 39 minutes. He showered, changed his clothes, and packed a bag for himself before he drove away.

Stephen and I looked at each other. I recalled the time when he'd said if police couldn't see it was murder, they'd never see.

I don't remember if Stephen said it, or if I did: "We're done. This investigation must end."

No one seemed surprised.

Curt asked if we planned to pursue a lawsuit.

"No, everything's finished."

Curt said: "Take the notebook."

Bless him. I took it.

It would be another year and a half until we succeeded in firing Nuch, however. As I studied the notebook, a story emerged about Dana's death, a story I'm trying to tell you. The notebook contained evidence of lies, inconsistencies, and foul play. For instance, police photos showed evidence of blood on a dining room chair, and dark, blood-like stains on the concrete floor of the master bath. I pointed these things out to Nuch. He communicated them to Bryan and to law enforcement.

Still, no one seemed to care.

These things happen. People are murdered, and murderers go unpunished. Sometimes, people are punished for murders they didn't commit. Justice is denied. Injustice is inflicted. The so-called Justice System seems incapable of offering a remedy. What difference does Dana's story make?

It's too late for justice for her, and for those of us who persist in calling attention to her case. Nonetheless, her story is worth telling, and worth hearing for its mix of screamingly obvious and perplexingly unusual circumstances.

2. REWIND

An episode of the television detective show *Columbo* aired on March 2, 1975. The episode was entitled "Playback." It told the story of a man who had installed closed-circuit television cameras in his posh Southern California mansion. The sophisticated cameras were activated by motion detectors and heat sensors, monitored in real time by a security guard. The system also recorded thick reels of video tape.

One night, the man shot his mother-in-law in his study. He manipulated the video system to manufacture an alibi. He put the recording of the murder on a delayed timer. He drove away from his mansion to attend a party at an art gallery, making sure the security guard and others would remember where he had gone and at what hour. While he was away from the house, the video system played back the tape of the shooting. The guard believed he was witnessing a murder in progress in real time. Meanwhile, the actual murderer was miles away with an airtight alibi. Police thought the victim had been shot by a mysterious intruder.

Lieutenant Columbo was skeptical. The presence of video cameras inside the mansion made him suspicious. He studied the video and saw a crucial clue that demolished the murderer's alibi. At the time of the shooting, on the man's desk was the invitation to the party he had attended at the art gallery. When the man left the mansion to go to the party, he had taken the invitation with him. Therefore, Columbo knew that the man had been in the mansion at the time of the murder.

Unlike the murderer in the *Columbo* episode who lived in a mansion in a monied enclave like Bel-Air, Huck and Dana lived in a relatively modest house on East Stearns Street, adjacent to a public golf course in the El Dorado Park neighborhood of Long Beach, California. My sister bought the house in 2001, several months after they married.

She was a successful kitchen designer who ran her own business from home. Huck was a general contractor. His finances had always been sketchy. Dana knew he would not qualify for a mortgage, so she bought the house herself. It was a 1950s ranch-style, single-family, detached home. It had potential, but it was cramped and outdated. The plan was for them to gain sweat equity by remodeling it themselves.

Huck's biography was as sketchy as his finances. Over the years, he told us several stories about his upbringing, but I don't know which ones were true. According to public records, Huck's mother Linda Kay Floyd married Huck's father David A. Martinez in November 1963 in Tacoma, Washington. Carl Lynn Martinez a.k.a. Huck was born in December 1964, and his parents divorced three years later.

Linda married Franklin Arnold "Rusty" Jenkins in 1971 in King County, Washington. At some point, public records suggest that they lived in Nampa, Idaho. A yearbook from Huntington Beach High School in California shows that Carl Lynn Jenkins a.k.a. Huck was a student there in 1980.

In 1986, Linda and Rusty bought a home on Surfbreaker Lane in Huntington Beach, a stone's throw from the golf course at Seacliff Country Club. Linda and Rusty separated and divorced in 1993. According to their divorce settlement, Linda kept the house on Surfbreaker Lane. Papers filed as part of the settlement show that Carl Jenkins lived with Linda in the home at that time. He was 28 years old. His gross monthly income was listed as "unknown." Property records show that the house on Surfbreaker Lane was sold in 1999, the year Huck met Dana.

To Dana, Huck portrayed himself as a carefree surf punk. Ever since her teen years, Dana had liked surfers. We grew up in Littleton, Colorado, which is about a thousand miles away from Southern California, and far from any ocean. In June 1977, when Dana was 14, I was 12, and my brother 10, my parents took us on a family trip to Disneyland. We visited Huntington Beach, too, and saw the immense, glittering Pacific Ocean for the first time.

In high school, Dana and I drove around the sleepy-and-boring suburbs of southwest Denver in a 1971 Volvo station wagon, which we could imagine one day carrying us and our surfboards along California's Pacific Coast Highway. We romanticized a wholesome, sanitized version of surf culture that we imagined from listening to pop songs by The Beach Boys. I can see how, decades later, my sister would similarly romanticize Huck. To her, he was a real-life beach boy.

Huck had problems with alcohol in his past, she told me, although he'd never specified what problems. He was not an alcoholic, he assured her, but he had sworn off alcohol because it made him do foolish things. Dana admired Huck for not drinking. She thought he must be very sensible.

My sister invited Huck to move into her condominium at Redondo Avenue and Third Street in Long Beach very soon after they started dating. She told me he was sleeping in his truck in an ex-girlfriend's garage. He would benefit from a stable, comfortable home, she believed; she invited him into hers.

Dana protected and defended Huck even at her own expense. At the condo, one of Dana's neighbors and friends hired him to do repair work on her condo. The woman was frightened by Huck's sudden, intense anger toward her and told Dana that he was abusive. Huck countered that the neighbor was making up stories because she was jealous of Dana's new romantic relationship. Dana and this woman had been close friends. They had gone on a Caribbean cruise together with the woman's family. Even so, Dana took Huck's side, rupturing her friendship with her neighbor.

I was living in a condo in West Hollywood on Kings Road just below Fountain Avenue. I had a minor renovation project I wanted to do. Dana suggested I hire Huck. He blew my electrical budget by installing several recessed lights in one small room. He said he had "tricked it out" for me, expecting me to be impressed. I complained to my sister that he had gone over budget on the lights. He hadn't done the electrical work I wanted him to do.

She said I must not have communicated clearly enough with him. Besides, the work he had done was good. I was lucky he was willing to drive all the way to West Hollywood to complete the remaining tasks.

He finished the work. I paid him more than I had planned. It was fine. No big deal.

Dana made excuses for him and protected him from consequences even when she thought his behavior was unacceptable. One 4th of July, Huck inexplicably started lighting firecrackers and dropping them off the balcony of Dana's condo onto passersby on the sidewalk below. She told him to stop but he didn't.

Later, he explained tearfully that the firecrackers were his inarticulate way of coping with painful childhood memories regarding his mother and her sisters. He spoke of his aunts as if they were vengeful gossips who enjoyed hurting him. He referred to them in the past tense, as if they were no longer alive. He became prickly and evasive when Dana asked for more details. Dana assumed he had endured horrific abuse that he was unable to discuss. She felt sorry for him, forgave him, and married him.

He cried during their wedding on November 24, 2000. At his insistence, no one from his family was invited to the ceremony. By that time, his mother Linda and stepfather Rusty were living together again in Sun City or Menifee, California. Huck claimed Linda was prone to making hurtful accusations about him and would not let him forget his past mistakes. He didn't want her making a scene at his wedding, and he hated Rusty, so they weren't invited.

Huck led us to believe that Linda and Rusty were his only living family members. Linda died in 2005, followed by Rusty in 2010. After that, Huck pretended he was all alone in the world, with no family except us Joneses.

Not until 2018 did I learn that Huck had aunts, cousins, and a grandmother living in Southern California. If these relatives had come up in a background check conducted by Nuch's team, it was never mentioned to me. I found out because our family genealogist researched Huck's family tree.

Two of Huck's friends were at the wedding. One was a fellow contractor named Tom Sawyer whom Huck had known since their youth. Their friendship had earned Carl Jenkins the nickname Huck Finn.

Huck's other friend was Paul Harrington. Huck shared a garage with Paul in Orange County, California. Paul ran a moving and storage business. Huck kept his construction truck at the garage and ran a struggling one-man company called True Construction. According to state licensing records, Huck established True Construction in 1995. Sometime after Dana bought the house on East Stearns Street in 2001, Huck moved his truck and his business to her driveway.

In 2004, Paul was arrested for illegally growing high-grade marijuana. According to news reports, police found 1,050 plants on the premises of Paul's business, as well as one pound of marijuana and a handgun in Paul's office. Police characterized Paul's grow operation as extensive. Electric service to the building had been altered. Paul was accused of stealing electricity to run irrigation equipment for his pot garden.

Huck told Dana and me that he was just as shocked as we were to learn of the criminal charges. In retrospect, I wonder who did the extensive plumbing and electrical work on Paul's pot garden.

At the conclusion of the wedding ceremony, Huck blubbered and wiped tears from his eyes. Dana thought this was sweet; it confirmed Huck's fragility and his joy at having a true family at last. I thought he was crying fake tears, and that he was doing it to upstage the bride and be the center of attention. This is a good example of how Dana and I disagreed fundamentally about the nature of Huck.

The ceremony and reception were held just off the coast of Marina Del Rey aboard motor yacht *Mauretania*, a graceful, 1930s-style yacht built in 1947. Dana had chosen it and had planned the party herself. It was a wonderful event, despite the groom. After

Dana's death, my dad chartered the same yacht. We sailed off Point Fermin near Long Beach and scattered Dana's ashes at sea. Huck wasn't invited to that ceremony; it was just for family.

Dana said she never felt threatened by Huck. I wonder if she told me this to spare me from imagining the worst. I once told her I thought Huck might physically hurt her. We ended up having an argument. She told me that he would never hurt her. He might raise his hand to their dog, or threaten self-harm, but he would never hurt her. She was certain of it.

For whatever reason, Huck didn't seem scary to her. She knew she was stronger than him emotionally. She had grit, and he didn't. His bullying seemed petty and manageable. If Dana confronted him, which she rarely did, he would cry and say he felt suicidal. He was just putting on a tough-guy act to protect himself, he would say.

As much as I disliked Huck, I was not aware, at least not consciously aware, that he had ever physically harmed my sister. Huck was muscular, certainly, and my sister joked that he was built like cartoon character Fred Flintstone. Even so, I thought his real strength was gaslighting, or undermining Dana's trust in her own accurate perceptions. Huck was great at it, and he did it all the time. He did it so frequently, and about such inconsequential things, that I stopped noticing it.

One example comes to mind. When he did the electrical work on my West Hollywood condo, he installed audio speakers, too. A couple of years later, after I had sold the condo and moved back to Colorado, he reminded me of the specific style of speaker he'd installed. He and I ended up arguing about it. I was sure that he misremembered the style of speaker. He insisted I was wrong, and he was right. He was so earnestly, sincerely adamant about it that I started to doubt my own memory. Was I crazy?

I ended up rifling through old photographs taken in my condo to find a picture of the actual speakers. I found one. Turns out, he was wrong, and I was right. I had a photo to prove it. I sent him a copy of the photo. Huck told Dana that only a "psycho bitch" would go to such lengths to prove a point.

There was nothing to be gained from engaging in a dispute with Huck, Dana had learned early in their relationship. Ordinary conversations with him could be exhausting because he seemed to need constant validation. Disputes were even more taxing. Eventually, my family and I learned to follow Dana's lead and go along with whatever story he told, whatever claim he made. I don't know if this qualifies as Stockholm Syndrome, but it did feel at times as if our whole family was held hostage by Huck.

It depresses me now to look at photos of Dana and Huck's house that were taken by the Long Beach police. To me, the photos show a house that gradually became dominated by Huck. As years passed, the house came to reflect Huck's taste for dark and sometimes ghoulish décor. He eventually walled off the front of the house so people couldn't see in from the street. He installed surveillance cameras inside and out.

I might have seen these things as signs of his escalating paranoia and deviousness. Instead, I assumed it was just Huck being his typical, inexplicable self. Back then, I wondered when my sister would admit that Huck was an emotionally manipulative burden on her, and file for divorce.

It wasn't always this way. For a time, their house had been a light, bright home full of possibilities. At moments, it seemed as if their marriage had a chance of being happy, mostly because Dana was determined to be happy no matter what.

The September 2006 issue of *This Old House* magazine featured a before-and-after article about Huck and Dana's home remodeling project. Over the years, several of Dana's kitchen designs had been featured in national magazines. She was thrilled to have her own home recognized in this way.

The article, which was written by Jill Connors, took note of the home's "concrete floors, engineered stone counters, and contemporary bamboo base cabinets." According to the article:

"Huck did much of the work, from gutting the room to the studs to running the electrical to staining the floors, which helped them stay within their $40,000 budget. Says Dana of the four-month kitchen redo, 'We needed to change everything about the space functionally and aesthetically—and we did.'"

In fact, the "four-month kitchen redo" took years because Huck did much of the work himself. It was a source of irritation for Dana that he dragged his feet on the kitchen project.

Eventually, the house looked fresh, well-finished, and modern in an unpretentious way. The dining chairs were a good example of this style. They were just plastic patio chairs, box resin outdoor dining armchairs by Compamia, to be exact, in bright orange. They were an inexpensive, practical way to add bold color to the dining area.

At her table, my sister hosted Thanksgiving dinner several times, even during the years when her kitchen languished in partially renovated limbo. As my family members will attest, the orange chairs weren't particularly comfortable. But they just seemed to fit the house.

Back then, if you were to see the house from the sidewalk, it looked cheerful and well-kept, with a front lawn and windows that looked out on a well-traveled street. Their lot was 0.10 acre in size, and the house was 1,322 square feet. Behind the house was El Dorado Park Golf Course, with trees and airy acres of grass, giving the house a feeling of spaciousness.

On March 4, 2014, police put an evidence marker near a pair of Huck's shoes, which were on the floor next to one of the bright-orange plastic chairs. Police photographed the shoes, but Detective Johnson apparently failed to notice blood spatter on the chair. I like to think that Lieutenant Columbo would have seen the blood, but he never showed up at my sister's house.

In 2018, four years after Johnson closed Dana's case, I saw a column written by retired Los Angeles Police Department Deputy Chief Stephen Downing, published in *Beachcomber*, a local paper in Long Beach. The column accused Detective Johnson of chronic, on-the-job alcoholism. A source told the columnist:

> "Todd Johnson was drunk or under the influence at work most of the time and everybody knew it."

The column alleged that Detective Johnson had been involved in a collision in a city-issued car after an evening of drinking in December 2017, and his supervisors covered up the incident. For years, according to the column, officers and supervisors in Long Beach had covered for Johnson's drunken sloppiness and explosive rage.

A different news report, written by Jeremiah Dobruck and published in the *Long Beach Press-Telegram* on April 23, 2018, recounted a murder investigation that Johnson had botched.

I had reason to wonder: Were Long Beach police honestly investigating Dana's death, or were they covering for a problematic detective known for botching homicide investigations?

In April 2018, I wrote to the Los Angeles District Attorney's Office to tell them about what I perceived to be Johnson's improper closure of Dana's case. The DA's office did not respond. In May 2018, I built a website at YogaDeath.com to publicize the case.

Through the website, I was contacted by a long-ago former girlfriend of Huck's. They had broken up, she said, but Huck was still living with her in 1999 when he met Dana. The woman told me her whirlwind romantic relationship with Huck had lasted just long enough for him to move into her condo. As quickly as their romance had started, it cooled, and Huck took up residence in her spare room. She said Huck became violent when she asked him to either start paying rent or move out. "You're ruining my life," he roared, overturning a table, and prompting her to lock herself in the bathroom for safety. She told me Huck had a felony conviction in his past that barred him from owning a gun, and yet he owned a gun.

I doubt Dana ever suspected Huck of having a criminal record. If Nuch's team had discovered this information, they hadn't told me. I wondered if the woman's story could be a hoax. I checked her name and past addresses. Sure enough, she and Huck had shared a past address.

I knew Huck owned at least one handgun because Dana had told me about it. Huck wanted to keep it under their bed. Dana told him to get rid of the gun or lock it in his safe.

In their garage, Huck kept a safe that was the size of a commercial refrigerator. He was proud of it. He told me it was from a former bank building that was being renovated. The safe gave me the creeps because it was big enough to fit a person inside it. Who needs or wants a safe like that, I thought, other than a drug dealer? I figured it was just another of Huck's tough-guy props, like the gun, a possession he thought made him seem cool, but for which he had no legitimate use.

Why do well-intentioned people make excuses for, defend, and protect people who repeatedly flash warning signs of destructive anger and deception? It's easier to rationalize it away than to confront it. It's easier to believe that a seemingly supportive husband would never kill his wife. A seemingly competent police detective would never deliberately misrepresent facts in a murder investigation.

After a while, you invest so much emotional capital and personal credibility rationalizing questionable behavior, it's too painful ever to acknowledge you've been conned. You just want to go on believing the best.

3. Film Noir

Huck's alibi, according to Johnson, was unassailable. He had taken the dog for a walk around the neighborhood on the morning of Monday, March 3, 2014. On surveillance video, he can be seen walking out the front door with the dog at 8:12 a.m. He can be seen returning to the house with the dog at 8:38 a.m.

Huck claimed that when he entered the house, he could hear Dana's iPad playing a yoga video behind the closed door of the yoga room. In surveillance video, Huck can be seen wearing earbuds as he entered the house. His ears remained covered for several minutes as he prepared a bed for the dog on a sofa. Huck told police that he heard a loud crash minutes after returning with the dog.

On the surveillance video, the dog on the sofa appeared to react to a noise at 8:48 a.m. Huck was not on camera at this time. Huck dialed 911 at 8:51 a.m. He did not reappear on camera until 8:56 a.m., when he exited the exterior door of the yoga room and opened the front gate.

During their search of the house on the night of Tuesday, March 4th, detectives seized Dana's iPad and the digital video recorder (DVR) from the home's video surveillance system. The system had been installed by Huck, and he was the only person who managed and monitored it. Nevertheless, detectives presumed video files on the DVR gave an authentic, complete account of activities in and around the house.

A limited forensic examination of Dana's iPad showed that it had been used to make a purchase from Levenger.com at 8:28 a.m. on March 3rd while Huck was away from the house. Minutes later at 8:33 a.m., the iPad was used to log in to a yoga instruction video on Gaia.com. The iPad played an episode of yoga teacher Rod Stryker's *Peak Performance Yoga*.

Detectives saw that Huck was not in the house at the times when Dana's iPad was used. Therefore, detectives assumed Dana was alive and well somewhere in the house using her iPad, even though she did not appear on camera that morning.

Huck could not have bludgeoned Dana and cleaned up the scene in just the nine minutes between the alleged "loud crash" that caused the dog to startle at 8:48 a.m., and the arrival of first responders at 8:57 a.m. Therefore, detectives presumed, as Huck had claimed, that Dana was alive and well in the house when he left to walk the dog. It seemed impossible that Huck could have assaulted her that morning; her injuries must've been the result of a terrible yoga accident.

When additional facts are considered, and when we watch the video, an alternate narrative begins to emerge. Based on this information, this is what I believe happened. Huck bludgeoned Dana on the night of Sunday, March 2, 2014, sometime after 10:21 p.m. in the master bathroom, where she bled profusely for hours overnight, mostly in the shower.

Huck used the pull-down ladder in the hallway to access the attic and the surveillance-system DVR. The device was located on the top shelf of the linen closet, just a few feet away from the attic hatch. The camera cords and power cables were within easy reach from the attic, and Huck temporarily disabled the system. While the cameras were off, Huck took Dana's iPad from the kitchen hutch.

Huck spent the night cleaning up blood and readying his alibi. Likely with help from a neighbor who was a former emergency-room nurse, Huck stopped the bleeding of the gaping wound in Dana's scalp, washed blood from her hair and dried it, dressed her, and placed her on the floor in the yoga room. In the morning, he re-activated the surveillance cameras.

Huck took Dana's iPad with him when he walked down the street with the dog. He walked to the golf-course footpath and doubled back in the direction of his house until he was within range of his home's Wi-Fi network. There, he used Dana's iPad and credit card to make an online purchase. He logged on to her

Gaia.com account and started playing the Rod Stryker yoga video.

Huck walked back the way he'd come, again carrying the iPad under his jacket, reappearing on camera with the dog. After he entered through the front gate of the house, he walked to the exterior door of the yoga room, removed the iPad from his waistband, and put the device outside the door. Through his Bluetooth earbuds, he could hear the Rod Stryker video as it played on Dana's iPad.

I'll walk through the video to show how it supports this narrative. But first, it's important to note multiple instances of digital-forensic malpractice and erroneous interpretation on the part of Long Beach police.

For example, the timestamp on the surveillance video in Dana's house was 24 minutes ahead of real time. This is not a big deal. Often, video timestamps do not reflect the accurate time. For this reason, as a matter of standard procedure, forensic video technicians make note of time discrepancies and write down details about the surveillance system's make, model, and settings.

In Dana's case, it's my understanding that this information was never collected. Bryan McMahon told me that he later calculated the time offset by looking at a wall clock recorded by Camera 6, presuming the clock on the wall to be correct. It's standard practice to calculate the time offset upon retrieval of the evidence, or to use a verifiable marker such as the arrival time of emergency vehicles. This is a relatively small matter, but it's indicative of slapdash work. Police failed to make note of the system's most basic details when they took it into evidence.

Another failure is that police did not retrieve any videos recorded by Camera 9. According to one police report, this camera was located somewhere near the exterior door of the master bedroom. Was this camera turned off or otherwise disabled? Did it record nothing? Were its recordings purposely not retrieved for some reason? A forensic video technician, following standard procedure, would have made note.

In Dana's case, police reports included a handwritten page specifying camera views associated with each video channel. Between the notes "CH 8 STREET VIEW SOUTH" and "CH 10 WEST SIDE OF RES/ S/W VIEW FRONT GATE," the note "CH 9" had been written and scribbled out as if listed by mistake. Unable to specify the view of Camera 9, police scratched it off the list as if it didn't matter.

These relatively minor mistakes and omissions hint at a larger problem. According to attorney Jonathan Hak, an international expert on forensic video analysis and the law, and the teacher of a training seminar I attended:

> "Relying on video evidence without expert interpretation risks the failure to reach the correct conclusions based on the evidence or worse, reaching the wrong conclusions."

Untrained detectives and unreliable "experts" who misinterpret digital media can very well botch an investigation, as I believe detectives did in Dana's case.

Police preserved only three clips of video from the night of Sunday, March 2, 2014. These clips cover just 21 minutes of real time. Based on these glimpses, police concluded that all was well in Dana's house.

That night, the broadcast of the 86th Annual Academy Awards, hosted by Ellen DeGeneres, had wrapped up just after 9:00 p.m. At 10:00 p.m., Huck walked out of the TV room and onto the back patio with the dog, a copper colored Viszla named Enzo. The air was a cool 54°F. Huck was barefoot and wearing shorts, but he also wore a hoodie sweatshirt.

Seconds after Huck walked outside, Dana walked away from the TV room and down the interior, central hallway of the house. Along this hallway were several rooms: Dana's office; the so-called yoga room; a laundry nook; and the master suite. There were no cameras in these rooms nor in the hallway. While the presence of 12 cameras initially gave detectives an impression of blanket surveillance, most of the home was hidden from view.

Enzo stayed outside with Huck for less than a minute. The dog sniffed at a patch of grass in the northeast part of the yard. Apparently triggered by the dog's activity, a motion-activated floodlight near the exterior door of the master bedroom came on briefly and went out. The floodlight was near the presumed location of Camera 9, which, if it was working, would have recorded this outdoor activity.

The dog went back inside the house. Huck followed.

Inside the house, Enzo went down the hallway, seemingly in search of Dana. He returned to the TV room moments later without her.

Huck, having taken off his hoodie, walked slowly from the TV room and through the dining area, past the orange chairs. Camera 6 recorded him going into the guest bathroom and closing the bathroom door. If Huck had turned on the bathroom light, it would have been visible through the frosted-glass panel of the door. He did not turn on the light.

Forty seconds later, Dana reemerged from the hallway. She had a troubled look on her face. She walked briskly past the glass door of the unlit bathroom, and into the TV room. Moments later, she appeared on the back patio with the dog.

My guess is that Enzo was barking or whining urgently, and this was why Dana looked troubled and walked briskly. Also, she was probably wondering where Huck had gone, and why he wasn't attending to Enzo.

Once outside, Enzo ran to the low wall at the back of the property. Dana hugged herself in the cool air. The dog wagged his tail as he stood at the wall, as if he wanted Dana to see something on the golf course. On top of this wall was a cable-rail fence which would have allowed Dana to see the footpath on the other side, and the misty darkness of the golf course in the distance. Neighbors often walked their dogs along the footpath.

Was a neighbor walking along the path? Did Dana exchange a greeting with someone? Whether she did or didn't, the video doesn't tell us. The camera's view of this area was blocked by a patio umbrella.

After a few moments, Enzo turned around and trotted back into the house. Dana followed. Huck was still in the bathroom in the dark.

Several seconds later, presumably in response to Dana calling for him, Huck opened the bathroom door. He peered around a corner and stood to face Dana. To me, this is an odd sequence. It appears as if Huck was hiding in the bathroom. He seemed hesitant to reveal himself.

When Huck set up the surveillance cameras, he had angled Camera 7 to cover the spot on which he was standing. To me, he looked uncomfortable under the camera's scrutiny. Dana stood off camera. Huck looked at her.

I would say that Huck glared at her. He turned his body toward the hallway as if wanting to get away. He raised his chin defiantly. Before he walked down the hall, he flashed a scowling double take at Dana. She followed him down the hall.

This sequence lasted only 10 seconds, but I find it enduringly puzzling. What was Dana saying to Huck during those awkward 10 seconds? I see uncomfortable tension between the two of them.

To a detective who didn't know Dana and Huck, this scene probably looked unremarkable. One of the detectives wrote a note: "Night before observe everyone. Dana/no apparent issues."

While the detective probably was not aware of festering issues in Dana's marriage, his note acknowledged crucial, indisputable information. Specifically, on this night, Dana did not show any signs of health issues, such as stumbling, confusion, lack of coordination, or lack of balance. She was not intoxicated. She did not behave erratically nor combatively. Nothing about her appearance hinted at the likelihood of an impending, fatal accident. Rather, she was wearing slippers, jeans, and a big sweater, and walking around her house with a serious expression on her face. In other words: "Dana/no apparent issues."

If police had examined videos from preceding nights, they would have been able to draw comparisons about the level of activity in the house on the last night of Dana's life. Police seized the entire digital video recorder from her house, after all. Detectives had weeks of surveillance videos at their fingertips.

This may sound like the beginning of thorough police work, but it's another cluster of mistakes. Unplugging a DVR and taking it to the police station to see what's on it should be done only as a last resort. Cutting the power to a DVR can cause it to malfunction or to erase itself when power is restored. Therefore, technicians customarily use a variety of techniques to retrieve video files without turning off the surveillance equipment.

Nonetheless, police unplugged the DVR and removed it from Dana's house. One of Nuch's investigators asked Detective Johnson if police conducted a forensic exam of the device. Johnson reportedly replied that a forensic exam wasn't necessary because there was no indication that the device had been tampered with or manipulated.

Of course, the only way to know whether it had been tampered with or manipulated would be to conduct a forensic exam.

Videos on the DVR could have given detectives insight into daily household routines, episodes of conflict, and the comings and goings of visitors. Investigators have told me that police did not retain copies of these videos. Bryan told me it would have been too burdensome for police to save more than a few hundred megabytes of digital files for Dana's case. Police saved everything that was relevant, Bryan said. This comprised three clips from the night of Sunday, March 2, covering approximately 21 minutes of real time, and 45 clips from the morning of Monday, March 3, covering approximately three hours of real time.

Without making a complete copy of the DVR, without even looking at everything on it, and without subjecting the surveillance system to a forensic examination, police gave the DVR back to Huck along with Dana's iPad, as if these weren't crucial bodies of evidence in a homicide investigation.

Why were police so derelict in their duty to scrutinize and retain evidence?

In 2018, I requested a copy of the LBPD's written policies and procedures for handling surveillance video. On February 11, 2019, Sergeant Joshua Brearley, Office of the Chief of Police, wrote to me in response:

> "The Long Beach Police Department does not have written policies specific to the retrieval or analysis of digital video evidence and CCTV."

Brearley wrote that the department had standards of practice for officers' body-worn cameras, but none for CCTV evidence. In other words, in Dana's case, police were winging it.

Even so, they did save bits and pieces of video, and these tell us something. For example, Dana walked in front of various cameras more than five times on the night of Sunday, March 2. She spent approximately nine minutes on camera standing at the kitchen hutch while using her iPad. Her level of activity on this night starkly contrasts with the following morning when cameras rolled for three hours but Dana never appeared on camera alive and well, not once, not ever.

When I watch the video from the last night of Dana's life, I see that she was concerned about something. Was she troubled by Huck's resurgent enthusiasm for drinking alcohol? His messy finances? A possible divorce? It could have been any of these worries, in addition to Huck's odd behavior that night, such as seemingly hiding in the guest bathroom in the dark.

A few minutes after the awkward scene in which Huck glared at her and she followed him down the hallway, Dana reappeared on camera. She turned on the light of the guest bathroom, went in, and closed the door. She was in the bathroom for approximately two minutes. She exited and turned off the light.

Moments later, she walked from the hallway to the kitchen hutch. At the hutch, she lifted the cover of her iPad.

Probably not by accident, the surveillance camera Huck had installed directly over the hutch, Camera 6, did not show the surface of the hutch. Rather, the camera was angled toward the front door. As Dana used her iPad, the camera recorded only a hint of the top of her head in the lower-right edge of the frame. This part of the frame was further obscured by the video timestamp.

Across the room, Camera 7 recorded Dana as she tapped on her iPad screen. The lights were low. The image is not as clear as I would like it to be. Still, it is unmistakable that Dana was using her tablet device.

After a minute at the hutch, Dana turned as if she had found the information she wanted and was walking away. She stopped. She drew her left hand to her mouth. Dana turned again to her iPad. She tapped on it for another eight minutes.

Was she sending an e-mail message? If so, we might never know what it said. The following morning, Huck sent messages from her main account to her friends and associates. Huck had every opportunity to read Dana's messages, and to delete whatever he wanted to erase.

A thorough forensic exam of the iPad might have been able to tell us what she was doing on the device that night. However, investigators have told me that police did not seek nor retain complete logs of her iPad and e-mail activity.

To conduct the forensic exam of Dana's iPad, it was necessary to unlock the device with a four-digit code. The forensic report shows the unlock code for the device was given to detectives, presumably by Huck because Dana was dead. Meaning, Huck was able to unlock and use Dana's iPad. His murder alibi relied on digital media evidence that he could access and manipulate, and yet this reality is never noted or analyzed by police.

Perhaps the most important moments in the night's video happened at the end. Dana walked away from her iPad, leaving it on the hutch. She walked across the room, down the hallway, and was gone. This was the last time she was recorded alive and well, and she was wearing eyeglasses. She needed them to see her iPad, and to watch a video on it. She didn't own contact lenses.

Police didn't find Dana's glasses in the yoga room. Rather, they found and photographed them in the master bathroom next to her sink. Likewise, police found and photographed Dana's iPad on the kitchen hutch exactly where she'd left it, far from the yoga room.

These details are important because they contradict Huck's alibi.

How could Dana have been watching a video in the yoga room if her glasses were in the bathroom, and she couldn't see the screen? How, exactly, did her iPad get into the yoga room if she did not carry it there? How, after her fatal "accident" did the device find its way back to the hutch, where police found and photographed it?

If, as detectives assumed, the surveillance system faithfully recorded all activity in and around the house without interruption, why was there no video showing who moved the iPad, and when?

After Dana walked off camera for the last time ever, eight hours went by with no videos to show for it. Police said there were no videos because nothing had happened in or around the house.

But, obviously, something happened. When Dana walked away, lights were on in the kitchen and dining area. A newspaper was in plain view on top of a hutch. But in the morning, the lights had been turned off, and the newspaper was gone. *Something* happened during the night. Why hadn't cameras recorded it?

Bryan speculated the lights were controlled by timer switches, and perhaps the cameras had malfunctioned when the newspaper was moved.

Bryan had no explanation for why all four exterior cameras in front of the house failed to work. These motion-activated cameras were pointed at busy East Stearns Street, yet they recorded nothing during the night. It's improbable that during an eight-hour span on Stearns, not one car drove past the house.

In 2016, my dad hired certified forensic video analyst Scott Alan Kuntz to examine video files from Dana's case and to answer some of my questions. I had attended a forensics seminar taught by Scott, who worked as a sheriff's deputy in Dane County, Wisconsin. Here's part of the written query I sent to Scott:

> ...My general theory is that Dana was fatally injured sometime between 10:20 p.m. on March 2nd, which is the last time she is seen alive and well on the video, and 6 a.m. on March 3. We have no videos covering this time period. However, several of the video files begin at around 6:34 a.m. on March 3. Is this because the CCTV system was switched off during the night, and was switched on at around 6:34? Is there another explanation for this gap in the recordings? ....

Here's part of Scott's response:

> What I don't know regarding the time gap is this:
>
> Did the police department only choose to export those files to the exclusion of others that might have been recorded throughout the night?
>
> Did the DVR have a programmed instruction to not record during the night? (Most DVRs allow the user to setup a 'schedule' of recording which is based on days of the week and times of day.)
>
> Did someone remove files from the DVR, which represented video files possibly recorded during the night? (In most DVRs, this would take extensive expertise to do successfully. This option would be improbable in most situations. Most consumer-grade DVRs allow a user to only format the entire hard drive but not selectively delete individual files.)

Does this model DVR stop recording when video signals are interrupted (power or video cables) to the DVR? If that is the case, it is possible that someone could have shut off power to all of the cameras late at night and then re-energized them in the morning. If the DVR and power supply weren't within camera view, this could produce a situation where no video files exist for the entire night. Someone could have re-energized the cameras or plugged their respective video cables back in without being seen on camera doing it. If the DVR behaves this way and if foul play is suspected, this would, in theory give a person the entire night to move about the house without being recorded on video.

If the DVR is still in police custody, a thorough forensic examination of the hard drive and of the DVR programming would help answer some of these questions…."

Scott also analyzed video file names and timestamps. He noticed details that raised additional questions about whether recordings were omitted by police, or by someone else. These details suggested that the cameras had been activated, and video files had been recorded during the night, but were missing from the cache of files preserved by police. Why were they missing?

Simply, police failed to gather and analyze a complete body of video evidence. We're left with doubts about what the video demonstrates. Police cannot claim credibly that the video shows proof of Huck's innocence. Likewise, it doesn't prove his guilt. It does, however, offer clues about Huck's role in what happened to Dana.

4. PLAYBACK

Dana's conspicuous absence on Monday morning is the most telling fact revealed by surveillance video. Over the course of three hours, while Huck was up and active throughout the house, Dana never appeared on camera. Why not?

Dana was a busy, self-employed kitchen designer with a waiting-list of clients. She worked from home. Her customary routine was to get up, do a quick series of yoga poses on the carpet next to her bed, prepare a cup of hot water with lemon, and start her day. She would scan her messages on her iPad. She would check her phone, which she usually plugged in and charged along with her iPad on the kitchen hutch. Why, on this morning, did she let hours tick by without even once looking at her phone?

Not only did Dana leave her iPad near the kitchen, she left her purse and wallet in the same spot. At 9:46 a.m., Camera 6 shows Huck taking Dana's phone from the kitchen hutch. At 10:13 a.m., Camera 6 shows Huck taking Dana's purse from the hutch and removing her wallet.

To get a credit card and make a purchase using her iPad, Dana would've had to appear on camera that morning at the kitchen hutch. But she didn't. She was noticeably absent.

I'll walk through the video to show what Huck did prior to calling 911. Remember, the video timestamp is 24 minutes ahead of real time. This offset was calculated by Scott based on the arrival time of first responders, which is a more reliable measure than the wall clock used by Bryan to verify real time. In this timeline, I cite the video timestamp and sometimes refer to the corresponding real time on March 3, 2014.

6:35 A.M., CAMERA 7

Many but not all cameras suddenly start recording around 6:10 a.m. real time. Huck and Enzo enter the dining area from the hallway. Huck hits a wall switch and turns on the light over the

32

dining table. He's barefoot, wearing a Quiksilver-logo t-shirt and shorts. Huck follows the dog into the TV room.

6:36 A.M., CAMERA 4

The dog walks across the back patio, followed by Huck. Huck is wearing Birkenstock sandals and a bulky, olive-drab coat now. Their activity in the backyard triggers the exterior light near the master bedroom door. Enzo returns to the house. Huck follows. This brief clip from 6:36 a.m. to 6:38 a.m. is the only recording made in the backyard all morning.

6:38 A.M., CAMERA 6

Still wearing his coat and sandals, Huck walks into the guest bathroom and closes the door. Enzo paces in circles.

6:39 A.M., CAMERA 7

Huck walks from the guest bathroom to the kitchen hutch. He opens the blinds of west-facing windows. Huck looks at the surface of the hutch where we saw Dana leave her iPad the night before. He touches the top of the hutch with his right hand. The surveillance video image is not large enough for us to see whether the iPad is still where Dana left it.

6:40 A.M., CAMERA 7

Huck walks into the kitchen. He opens the blinds of the front window, which is located over the kitchen sink. When Huck stands at the sink, facing directly south, he can see the front yard and East Stearns Street. To the left of the sink and just above the cooktop is an east-facing window that looks out across the enclosed front patio toward the exterior door of the yoga room.

This exterior door features a window in the center and is flanked by narrow windows. A mirrored closet door inside the room is directly opposite the exterior door. Windows and mirrors make the interior of the yoga room visible to someone standing outside on the enclosed front patio.

Prior to Dana's death, I never heard anyone refer to this room as the "yoga room." Rather, it was once a guest bedroom where, for some months of their marriage, Huck slept apart from Dana.

Around 2009, Huck installed the exterior door. He tore out the carpet and covered the exposed concrete floor with black stain. He bought a punching bag and practiced mixed martial arts. It was called Huck's workout room. He hung a collection of ghastly Japanese masks depicting demon faces on the south wall. Dana didn't like them. She asked Huck to install a curtain so she could easily cover the masks when she wished.

To my knowledge, Dana did not use this room for her yoga practice. Her brief, morning routine was something she could do anywhere, in a relatively small space, even in the cabin of a cruise ship. On some afternoons and evenings, she liked to attend yoga classes. Because she worked from home, she looked forward to going out for yoga because it was a good reason to get away from the office. She didn't need a "yoga room."

Similarly, she didn't need to follow a yoga video to do her morning routine. She had been practicing for many years. She often encouraged me, as well as Huck, to start practicing. She gave me a gift subscription to Gaia.com at Christmas 2013, hoping I would be inspired by the videos. Since her death, I have watched Rod Stryker's *Peak Performance Yoga* several times. It's a slow, sedate program to guide beginners through standard poses. Dana was well beyond it.

Throughout the morning, we'll see Huck spend a lot of time in the kitchen looking out the windows. He repeatedly wipes the cooktop and counters. From this location, he can keep an eye on both the yoga room and the front of the house.

6:45 A.M., CAMERA 7

The dog eats a bowl of food in the kitchen. When he's finished, the dog walks east down the hallway. To return to the west side of the house, the dog has two options. He can retrace his steps and come back up the hallway into the dining area, in which case he would be recorded by Cameras 6 and 7. Or he can exit the door of the master bedroom, walk across the back patio, and enter through the TV room, which would be recorded by Camera 4.

We'll see that the next time the dog appears on camera, at 7:36 a.m., he emerges from the TV room. This shows that, somehow, the dog can travel from one side of the house to the other without appearing on camera. If Enzo the dog can move around the house without being recorded, Huck can, too.

6:55 A.M., CAMERA 7

Still wearing his coat, Huck spends 15 minutes in the kitchen looking out the front windows as if waiting for someone to arrive. He prepares a beverage. Holding a cup, Huck walks through the dining room and into the TV room. Forty minutes will pass before he is again on camera.

7:15 A.M., CAMERA 8

Huck's friend and neighbor pulls up in a white SUV. She parks at the curb in front of Huck's house. This woman is a former emergency-room nurse named Marian with whom Huck has a close relationship. Later, Marian will tell police that she helped Huck clean up Dana's blood. She lives two doors down from Huck. The golf-course footpath behind their houses allows them to travel from one house to the other.

When Marian pulls up to the curb, it's just before 7:00 a.m. real time. Why did she park in front of Huck's house rather than in her own driveway? Had she left to run an errand? Marian picks up something from the passenger seat before she exits her vehicle. She is recorded by Cameras 2, 5, and 8 walking down the sidewalk to her house.

7:35 A.M., CAMERA 7

Huck walks from the TV room into the dining area. He's wearing his coat and Birkenstock sandals, as if he has been outdoors. He's also wearing reading glasses. He places **his** iPad— he has one separate from Dana's—on the dining table. He walks to the kitchen window where he can see Marian's car at the curb.

7:36 A.M., CAMERAS 6 AND 7

After looking out the front windows, Huck walks from the kitchen back to the dining table. He picks up his iPad. At the same moment, Enzo reappears on camera, entering the dining area from the TV room. The dog trots east down the hallway. Fifty-four minutes will pass before the dog again appears on camera.

Huck takes his iPad into the guest bathroom and closes the door. On Camera 6, there's an unexplained 10-minute gap between when Huck closes the bathroom door and when the door is open. He was not recorded leaving the bathroom, so we do not know exactly when he exited.

7:47 A.M., CAMERA 7

While Camera 6, for whatever reason, was not recording the bathroom door, Huck is seen on Camera 7 placing his iPad on the hutch located near the hallway. He suddenly leans out of the hallway, places the device on the hutch, and disappears again down the hallway.

What's happening in the hallway? Remember, this is where the pull-down ladder to the attic is located. This attic ladder would give Huck access to the surveillance DVR, which is located on the top shelf of the linen closet opposite the guest bathroom.

Meanwhile, a video can be seen playing on the screen of Huck's iPad. The image resembles a human figure moving slowly. It's possible that the device is playing a yoga video much like Rod Stryker's *Peak Performance Yoga*. It's possible that Huck previewed the yoga video that he would later claim as part of his alibi.

7:48 A.M., CAMERA 7

Huck walks into the dining area from the hallway. He picks up his iPad from the hutch and takes off his reading glasses. He switches off the iPad's screen display and places the device on the dining table. He places his glasses on the iPad. He produces a cell phone from somewhere off camera and places it on the iPad.

7:49 A.M., CAMERA 7

Huck walks to the kitchen. He stands at the sink for several minutes. While he's there, his phone on the dining table lights up with a notification, which he ignores.

7:54 A.M., CAMERAS 1, 3, 5, AND 7

This is a curious sequence. At the sink, Huck fills a glass with liquid. He walks from the kitchen out the front door. He looks at the yoga room as he opens the front gate. He apparently dumps out the liquid in the glass. He looks southeast at Camera 5, which is mounted on a lamppost in the yard. He returns to the front patio and closes the gate behind him. With an anxious expression, he looks up at Camera 1. As he walks toward the front door with the empty glass in his hand, he looks anxiously at the yoga room.

What's going on here? I suspect Huck has a helper cleaning up blood and staging the scene. Huck is worried, perhaps, that this person's movements might be recorded inadvertently by the cameras. Perhaps Huck went through this exercise with the glass of liquid so he could check his front cameras to be sure they were pointing where he wanted them to point.

Many of the cameras are positioned to capture an oddly narrow view. For instance, if the cameras were for home-security purposes, it would make sense for Camera 1 to show the entire exterior door of the yoga room as well as the front gate. These are two points of entry for a burglar, after all, and both points could be covered by the same camera. But Huck has narrowed the view to show just a small part of the patio in front of the yoga room door, plus the front gate.

7:55 A.M., CAMERA 7

Huck leaves the front door wide open when he walks back into the house. He returns to the kitchen. He puts the now-empty glass in the dishwasher. He again wipes down the counters and cooktop as he gazes out the windows. All his scrubbing and wiping reminds me of Lady Macbeth's unconscious laundering of her murder guilt; "Yet here's a spot... Out, damned spot! Out, I say!"

7:56 A.M., CAMERAS 1, 3, AND 6

Huck abruptly walks out the front door. This time he marches directly to the exterior door of the yoga room. Huck moves a wood-framed loveseat. He appears to pick up two panels of white, foam-core insulation. We can see Huck's feet as he stands outside the yoga room for several seconds. Is he talking to someone? He walks toward the front door. He casts an anxious look back at the yoga room.

7:57 A.M., CAMERAS 3, 6, AND 7

Huck carries the panels of insulation into the house, through the dining area, and into the TV room. Later, police will photograph these specific insulation panels in the garage. The same police photo shows the interior of the garage door lined with this same brand of insulation.

How and why were these panels in or near the yoga room? What accounts for Huck's sudden urgency to move these panels?

My guess is these panels were in the attic. One piece looks as if it would fit over the linen closet where the DVR is located. The other looks as if it would fit over the laundry nook, where the home's Internet router and other electronics are located. Perhaps these panels were removed to make it easier to access cords and cables via the attic. Huck couldn't leave the panels in or near the yoga room, perhaps, because he knew first responders would be coming later that morning. The panels might trigger questions or get in the way.

7:58 A.M., CAMERAS 6 AND 7

Huck appears to be carrying empty cups and glassware as he returns to the kitchen from the TV room. Has he had company? With his left arm, he shuts the front door. He puts dishes into the dishwasher and gazes out the front window. He opens the refrigerator a couple of times and appears to be making something at the sink. He washes the dog's bowl.

8:01 A.M., CAMERA 7

Huck looks out the east widow in the direction of the yoga room. He appears to hesitate, doing a double take. We see him shrug, smile, and shake his head. At the dining table, he puts on his reading glasses and checks his cell phone. He can see the notification he received earlier at 7:25 a.m. real time. He puts down the phone, removes his glasses, and exits into the TV room.

8:02 A.M., CAMERA 7

Huck returns from the TV room carrying a plastic jug. He walks to the kitchen. He appears to fill the jug at the kitchen sink. Later, Marian will tell police she helped Huck clean up Dana's blood using a solution of warm water, bleach, and Simple Green. Huck carries the jug into the TV room and off camera.

8:05 A.M., CAMERAS 6 AND 7

Huck returns from the TV room without the jug. He stops at the coffee table, which is just south of the dining table. He puts his feet, one at a time, on the coffee table and examines his Birkenstock sandals. Later, police photos of the master bathroom will show sandal tread prints stamped in stains on the floor. Huck walks into the kitchen and again looks out the front windows. At 8:07 a.m., he walks into the TV room and off camera.

8:28 A.M., CAMERA 7

For the past 21 minutes, no activity has been recorded inside the house. Ten hours have passed since Dana was last seen alive and well in her own home. Sunlight fills the house now, so the indoor cameras record in color. Huck walks to the dining table from the TV room. He has taken off his coat. He's wearing a bright orange t-shirt. He's barefoot and appears to be breathing heavily. He puts on his eyeglasses and checks his phone. At 8:29 a.m., Huck walks down the hallway toward the yoga room.

8:30 A.M., CAMERA 7

Huck returns from the hallway carrying a change of clothes. He's carrying camouflage shorts in his right hand and a green t-shirt in his left. He walks into the TV room.

8:31 A.M., CAMERA 7

Enzo the dog enters the dining area from the hallway. The dog was last seen on camera at 7:36 a.m. Where has Enzo been all this time? He walks into the TV room.

8:33 A.M., CAMERA 7

Closely followed by the dog, Huck walks out of the TV room and into the dining area. He is wearing camouflage shorts, socks, shoes, and a dark coat covered with a pixelated camouflage pattern.

Why did Huck change his clothes in the TV room rather than in the master bedroom or bath? Later, police photos will show a pile of Huck's clothes on a chair in the TV room, and a blanket on the sofa. It's possible that, as had happened previously in their marriage, Huck was not sleeping with Dana in the master bedroom. Rather, it's possible that he was sleeping on the sofa in the TV room.

Huck picks up his cell phone from the dining table and puts it in his pocket. He walks into the guest bathroom and closes the door.

8:33 A.M., CAMERA 5

At the same time Huck enters the guest bathroom, his neighbor Marian walks out of her house. She pauses on the sidewalk. All morning, a construction crew has been doing repair work on Stearns Street west of her house. The construction workers, most of whom appear to be wearing orange t-shirts, have been walking up and down the sidewalk in front of Huck's house. Marian looks in the direction of the repair work. She turns and walks toward her car. She appears to be carrying bags over her shoulders.

8:34 A.M., CAMERAS 2 AND 8

Marian pulls away from the curb and into slow traffic heading west on Stearns.

8:35 A.M., CAMERAS 6 AND 7

Huck exits the guest bathroom. He's now wearing sunglasses with attached Bluetooth earbuds covering his ears. He pauses at the dining table near his iPad, touches his ears, and walks to the kitchen. He looks out the front window. He can see Marian's car is no longer parked in front of his house. He looks west down the street in the direction she has driven. He lingers at the window. He puts a collar on the dog and again looks out the window. He grabs the dog's leash and returns to the window. Huck puts the leash on the dog.

8:36 A.M., CAMERAS 1, 3, AND 5

At 8:12 a.m. real time, with the Enzo on a leash, Huck walks out the front door and out the front gate. He walks to one of the raised flower beds in the front yard. Moments after he walks to the flower bed, Camera 5 switches on. Twenty seconds after the camera is activated, Huck leads Enzo to the sidewalk. Camera 5 shows them walking west on Stearns, in the same direction Marian drove just three minutes earlier.

Ten houses down on Huck's block in the direction he's walking, there's an open lot that allows public access to the footpath along the golf course behind Huck's house. I suspect that he's carrying Dana's iPad under his camouflage-pattern jacket. He knows Marian isn't home because he has seen that her car is gone. I think it's likely that he walks to the open lot, doubles back to Marian's house along the footpath and, once in range of a Wi-Fi network he can access, he uses Dana's iPad.

According to police, the iPad is used at 8:28 a.m. real time to buy a purse on Levenger.com. While Huck is away, no activity is recorded inside the house. Dana has not appeared on camera all morning. At 8:33 a.m. real time, her iPad is used to log on to the Rod Stryker *Peak Performance Yoga* video on Gaia.com.

Later, Randy Candias, one of Nuch's investigators, will tell me he spoke to Gaia.com about Dana's account. Months after Dana's death, Randy learned, someone continued to log on to her account and watch videos. Meaning, someone other than Dana was able to access her account, and I'm guessing that person was Huck.

9:03 A.M., CAMERAS 1, 8, AND 10

Huck appears on camera with Enzo. It's now 8:39 a.m. real time. Six minutes have passed since the yoga video started playing on Dana's iPad. I suspect that, through his Bluetooth earbuds,

Huck can hear Rod Stryker's voice narrating the video. With a garden hose near the front gate, Huck sprays the front walk. Later, he will tell police that he is washing his shoes and Enzo's feet.

9:05 A.M., CAMERAS 1 AND 3

When Huck and Enzo enter the front gate, the dog runs west toward the front door. Huck calls him back and leads him east toward the exterior door of the yoga room. We can see Huck lift his jacket, as if adjusting the waistband of his shorts. He walks toward the patio furniture directly in front of the yoga room. Later, police photos will show a small table between the two patio loveseats. This table is just out of view of the surveillance camera. I suspect that Huck removes Dana's iPad from his jacket and places on this table. We can see Huck's feet as he stands briefly outside the yoga room.

9:06 A.M., CAMERA 3

Enzo runs to the front door. Huck follows. Huck spends a long minute rubbing down the dog with a white cloth. This cloth was resting on the loveseat cushions, which are near the front door. It looks as if the cushions had been washed and were propped up to dry. After drying the dog, Huck puts the towel on the cushions.

9:07 A.M., CAMERAS 6 AND 7

Huck and Enzo enter the house through the front door. Enzo runs to the hallway but turns around and runs to the kitchen. Indoors, Huck is still wearing the sunglasses with attached earbuds. He places his cell phone on the kitchen hutch and stands at the front window. He feeds something to the dog. Huck takes off his jacket and walks with it to the TV room. He's wearing a green t-shirt. He continues to wear his sunglasses.

9:08 A.M., CAMERAS 6 AND 7

Huck walks from the TV room down the hallway. About 15 seconds later, he returns with an armload of bedding. Huck covers the sofa with sheets and prepares a bed for Enzo. To me, the dog seems sad. This preparation and protection of the sofa is something Huck and Dana would do when they planned to leave the dog home alone for more than an hour. The whole time, Huck is wearing sunglasses with earbuds.

9:09:45 A.M., CAMERA 7

Huck walks toward his laptop computer, which, according to police photos, is on the dining table but unseen by surveillance cameras. At this moment in the yoga video, Rod Stryker says, "Triangle pose." As if on cue, Huck abruptly pushes an orange dining chair under the table. At last, he takes off his sunglasses. Later, a police photo will show the sunglasses on a yellow note tablet on the dining table next to a stack of papers marked with State Farm Insurance logos.

Huck casts a glance over his shoulder. He walks off camera into the TV room.

To me, the dog seems confused. After Huck walks off camera, Enzo stands in the dining area for 30 seconds before turning and walking down the hallway toward the yoga room. He doubles back, goes into the TV room, comes out of the TV room and stands by the dining table.

9:11 A.M., CAMERAS 6 AND 7

This is the clip that Bryan McMahon showed me, the one that he said exonerated Huck. Huck enters the dining area from the TV room. He walks to his iPad, which is still on the dining table. He puts on reading glasses and taps on the screen of the device. After a minute of looking at the screen, he turns off the display, removes his reading glasses, and leaves them on top of the iPad.

Next, he does something extraordinary. Huck runs his fingers through his hair. He walks to the center of the room and looks at himself in the mirror above the sofa. Huck grooms his hair in the mirror. He looks at his profile, turning his head from one side to the other. He raises his right hand to his right cheek, and with a caress of his face, he spins around and marches down the hallway.

Enzo follows Huck down the hallway. Fifteen seconds later, Enzo returns. As if commanded, the dog gets on the bed Huck has made for him on the sofa. Three seconds later, at timecode 9:12:34 a.m., Enzo raises his head and looks toward the hallway. Looking puzzled, the dog remains on the sofa.

This, according to police, is the exact moment when Dana supposedly fell out of a risky yoga pose and cracked her head on a bare concrete floor. In real time, it's 8:48:34 a.m., which corresponds to 15 minutes and 34 seconds into *Peak Performance Yoga*. At this exact point in the video, the yoga practitioner is merely standing on her yoga mat, breathing deeply and, in the words of Rod Stryker, feeling "vibrant and alive."

Ten seconds after Enzo raises his head, Huck steps out of the hallway. He looks at the dog. Huck turns to his right to face the camera. Huck acts as if he's brushing his teeth. He walks down the hallway and off camera. Two minutes will pass before Huck calls 911.

5. DIRTY CALL

Sometimes the person who calls 911 to summon help for a dead or dying person is the one responsible for the person's death. Guilty callers often sound different than innocent callers, and they inadvertently say things that indicate their guilt. This is not merely a matter of subjective interpretation. There are objective criteria for evaluating statements made by 911 callers.

Susan H. Adams and Tracy Harpster wrote a textbook entitled *Analyzing 911 Homicide Calls: Practical Aspects and Applications* (CRC Press/Taylor & Francis, 2017.) The authors analyzed a thousand homicide calls to emergency dispatchers over a 12-year period. The cases they analyzed were clearly adjudicated. Meaning, questions of guilt and innocence regarding the callers had been formally weighed by the justice system. Based on their research, Adams and Harpster developed a checklist for evaluating whether a caller's statements indicated innocence or guilt.

Research showed that innocent callers immediately demanded help for the victim, such as saying, "I need an ambulance really quick." Innocent callers tended to focus on the victim, and to assess the victim's condition, saying things such as, "We have a resident who is lying on the floor and he feels cold to the touch." Innocent callers tended to provide aid to the victim, and to cooperate with the dispatcher. Innocent callers tended to volunteer sensory descriptions, and to gush relevant information about the situation. The tone of voice of innocent callers tended to be urgent, demanding, and even aggressive at times.

Guilty callers, on the other hand, often made no immediate plea for help for the victim. Guilty callers tended to offer extraneous information, such as statements about where they had been, or what they had been doing. For example, a husband called to report finding his wife dead in the backyard, saying: "I just got home from a baseball game." In this example, mentioning the baseball game had nothing to do with the victim, and everything to do with establishing the killer's alibi.

Rather than urgently volunteering details and cooperating with the dispatcher, guilty callers tended to use a variety of tactics to resist the dispatcher, such as evasion, equivocation, repetition, and self-interruption. Guilty callers tended to offer conflicting facts, and to use awkward phrases. They often spoke with little variation in the tone or pitch of their voices.

Guilty callers also tended to have unexplained knowledge about the situation. For example, a man who allegedly came home and found his wife dead told the dispatcher, "My wife has been stabbed 13 times." Unless he had committed or witnessed the murder, it's unlikely that he would know how many times she had been stabbed.

Here's a transcript of Huck's 911 call. To the left of the speaker's name is the time that the statement was made within the context of the recording.

[00:00] Electronic voice of time/date stamp: Monday, March 3rd, 2014. The time 8:51 a.m.

[00:08] Dispatcher: Long Beach Fire Department and Paramedics. What's the address of your emergency?

[00:11] Huck: 7053.

[00:13] Dispatcher: What street?

[00:14] Huck: East-East Stearns Street.

[00:16] Dispatcher: OK. Is this a house or an apartment? What is that?

[00:18] Huck: It's my home. It's my home.

[00:19] Dispatcher: OK. And is this for you or for someone else?

[00:22] Huck: It it's for my wife. She was doing yoga, doing a headstand, fell, and she's, um, bleeding from behind.

[00:26] Dispatcher: How old is she?

[00:27] Huck: Uh, fifty.

[00:29] Dispatcher: OK. She's bleeding from the back of her head, or?

[00:31] Huck: Yes. Yes.

[00:32] Dispatcher: OK, did she go unconscious at all?

[00:34] Huck: Yes.

[00:35] Dispatcher: She did pass out, yes?

[00:37] Huck: Yes. Yes.

[00:38] Dispatcher: Listen, help is coming. Stop yelling at me. OK. I'm trying to help you. Is she alert and aware of what's going on right now?

[00:44] Huck: Um, vaguely. She—you could tell she's concussed for sure.

[00:48] Dispatcher: OK. How's her breathing? Any difficulty breathing?

[00:50] Huck: I'm holding her and everything's fine, and the pulse seems to be calm and steady.

[00:55] Dispatcher: OK, OK, so can you lay her down, though?

[00:57] Huck: Um, I, I tried. It's a little combative. So I'm holding her, um, vertic—not not. She's sitting but I'm holding her upright [unintelligible.]

[1:04] Dispatcher: OK. So she was doing a head, like a handstand when it happened?

[1:08] Huck: Correct.

[1:09] Dispatcher: OK, did you see her, well, did you see her when it happened by any chance?

[1:13] Huck: Uh, no. I just heard a loud crash and came running into the room.

[1:15] Dispatcher: OK, do we know if she, if there's a possibility of her having a neck injury, like her twisting it, or a back injury?

[1:21] Huck: I'm gonna say, um, at this stage, right now, no.

[1:25] Dispatcher: OK. OK. Alright. Uh. I need you to keep a, a very close eye on her breathing and her alertness for any changes, OK. How heavily is her head bleeding?

[1:34] Huck: Uh, massive.

[1:35] Dispatcher: OK. Is there, do you have a clean, dry cloth or a towel, or something you can grab?

[1:39] Huck: I can't, I can't leave her alone, so I have a yoga towel around her, but I can't get anything else, um, I can't leave her alone.

[1:44] Dispatcher: You don't have anything you can tie like a tourniquet, right?

[1:47] Huck: Uh, no, no, no not around her [unintelligible.]

[1:49] Dispatcher: OK. OK. It's like a yoga towel that's like a hand-towel-sized thing?

[1:54] Huck: Yes.

[1:54] Dispatcher: OK. Take that, put—

[1:55] Huck: I'm applying pressure but at some point I have to unlock the gate.

[1:58] Dispatcher: OK. Just keep an eye on her. Keep your phone with you. If she gets worse…

[02:01] Huck: OK I—

[02:02] Dispatcher: …before we get there, call back on 911. OK? They're on the way.

[02:06] Huck: Alright. Bye.

The most immediate indicator of Huck's guilt is the fact that he never asked for assistance of any kind. He never requested an ambulance. Thirty seconds ticked by before anyone mentioned help, when the dispatcher said, "Listen, help is coming." Huck never said the word help.

To me, this is a clear indication that Huck was not calling for help. I believe that, from Huck's perspective, there was no emergency. Rather, Huck was calling primarily for the purpose of framing the situation: his wife had been doing yoga, and she had hurt herself somehow.

It was like pulling teeth for the dispatcher to extract details from Huck. She asked: "What's the address of your emergency?" He responded: "7053." He waited for the dispatcher to ask: "What street?" Huck said the name of the street. The dispatcher asked if it was a house or an apartment. Huck responded: "It's my home. It's my home." This didn't answer the dispatcher's question, and the repetition of the statement was another unnecessary delay. At this point, Huck had given the dispatcher no information about what his "emergency" might involve.

She asked: "Is this for you, or for someone else?"

At last, 14 seconds into their exchange, Huck told the dispatcher: "It it's for my wife. She was doing yoga, doing a headstand, fell, and she's, um, bleeding from behind."

Notice how he prioritized the information. His top priority was to establish the framing that his wife was doing yoga. She had hurt herself doing yoga. No one had done anything to her; she had done it to herself. If anyone was to blame, she was.

Next, Huck used a peculiar turn of phrase: "She's, um, bleeding from behind." This doesn't sound grave or life-threatening because it's hard to guess what it might mean. People are hit from behind or ambushed from behind. But "bleeding from behind" is not a phrase that anyone uses.

When he said, "bleeding from behind," Huck inadvertently hinted at what had really happened, I believe: Dana had been assaulted from behind. Huck's total lack of urgency in his communication with the dispatcher suggests to me that this assault from behind was not an emergency because it had not occurred in the minutes just prior to his call. Rather, I believe, it had happened several hours before he called 911.

At this point in the call, the dispatcher knew only that the victim was "bleeding from behind," and had to guess what this meant. For the next 10 seconds, the dispatcher tried to find out how serious the victim's condition was. She asked a series of questions that Huck answered with only one or two words.

Adams and Harpster describe this pattern as "Only Answers What's Asked." According to their research, this is a method of resisting the dispatcher, and it is a strong indicator of guilt. Callers who used this pattern of communication often resembled "hostile witnesses being questioned in the courtroom, after receiving legal advice to answer only what's asked." In their research, "over a quarter of all the calls (26 percent) contained this method of resistance, which was almost exclusively used by guilty callers (94 percent versus six percent.)" In other words, 94 percent of the time, callers who only answered what was asked were guilty.

The dispatcher, not understanding the nature of the situation due to Huck's resistance, sought to clarify: "She did pass out, yes?"

Huck responded with aggravation in his voice, as if the dispatcher was being obtuse: "Yes. Yes."

The dispatcher retorted: "Listen, help is coming. Stop yelling at me. OK. I'm trying to help you."

The dispatcher must have been frustrated by Huck's resistance. Still, it's important to note that Huck did not yell. His tone was taciturn and annoyed, but he didn't yell. It's interesting to me that when accused of yelling, Huck didn't argue in his defense. My sense is that he was trying extra-special hard to say as little as possible to avoid incriminating himself. Therefore, I think, he didn't dispute the dispatcher's mischaracterization of his tone.

Also, it's worth reiterating that, according to Adams and Harpster, innocent callers in an emergency tend to be demanding and even aggressive in their tone. Huck was neither. On the contrary, he sounded brusque, as if being inconvenienced by the dispatcher.

The dispatcher asked: "Is she alert and aware of what's going on right now?"

Huck replied: "Um, vaguely." He had to think about his answer, inserting "um" to buy time. The word "vaguely" is an equivocation; it's the rhetorical equivalent of saying yes, no, and maybe at the same time.

Next, he interrupted himself, saying, "She—you could tell she's concussed for sure." To me, it sounded as if he was going to make a definitive statement about her condition, starting with the word "she." But he interrupted himself and went in a different direction: "you could tell she's concussed for sure." While this might sound like a definitive statement because he said "for sure" at the end, it's a distant, impersonal assessment. Notice that **he** could not say she was concussed. Rather, **you** could tell she's concussed. When confronted with a direct question from the dispatcher, he gave a vague answer.

The dispatcher pressed for more information: "How's her breathing? Any difficulty breathing?"

Huck replied, "I'm holding her and everything's fine, and the pulse seems to be calm and steady."

Everything's fine. He minimized the situation, signaling to the dispatcher that whatever had happened, it wasn't serious.

The dispatcher sounded as if she understood at last that the situation was not urgent, saying: "So can you lay her down, though?"

Huck immediately contradicted what he had just said: "Um, I, I tried." (When did he try this, I wonder? Prior to calling 911?) "It's a little combative. So I'm holding her, um, vertic—not not. She's sitting but I'm holding her upright [unintelligible.]"

In other words, no, he would not comply with the dispatcher's reasonable suggestion to lay the victim down because, somehow, everything was not fine when he tried.

Try to picture it. He has a phone in one hand and is holding Dana in a seated position. If he does not maintain this position, and instead tries to lay her down, she fights him somehow.

Dana's voice cannot be heard in the 911 audio. Her silence tells me that she was so severely injured that she could not speak or cry out and could not even moan. I wonder how, then, she managed to be combative.

The dispatcher attempted to understand the situation: "So she was doing a head, like a handstand when it happened?"

Huck answered as if on the witness stand: "Correct."

The dispatcher asked: "Did you see her, well, did you see her when it happened by any chance?"

Huck answered: "Uh, no. I just heard a loud crash and came running into the room."

This is a telling statement. First, it's a demonstrable lie. According to the surveillance video, he did not go running into the room after allegedly hearing a loud crash; rather he stood in the dining area and appeared to brush his teeth. Second, it's a partial truth in the sense that, truthfully, he did not see her when she fell while doing yoga. He didn't see it because it didn't happen. Third, this statement reaffirms Huck's purpose for making the call: to assert his alibi that something happened to the victim, but he didn't do it. He couldn't have done it because he wasn't even in the same room with her when it happened.

The dispatcher, still seeking to understand, asked: "Do we know if she, if there's a possibility of her having a neck injury, like her twisting it, or a back injury?"

Huck responded: "I'm gonna say, um, at this stage, right now, no."

He offered no sensory description of the victim to explain why or how he reached this conclusion. He wanted the dispatcher to believe that the victim's head had been injured in a fall. Therefore, he waved the dispatcher away from thinking about other scenarios, and other possibilities. Note the equivocation and stalling as he contemplates his answer: "I'm gonna say, um, at this stage, right now, no."

What stage was he referring to? How many "stages" of this situation had already occurred, and, in his mind, how many stages were yet to come?

The dispatcher continued: "I need you to keep a, a very close eye on her breathing and her alertness for any changes, OK. How heavily is her head bleeding?"

Huck replied: "Uh, massive."

He kept this information to himself for a full minute and a half. Imagine: you find a loved one at home on the floor, bleeding massively from a head wound, yet when you call 911, you neglect to mention this detail until prompted. According to Adams and Harpster, innocent callers immediately assessed the victim, informing the dispatcher of massive head injuries and profuse bleeding within the first several seconds of the call.

Funny thing, though: according to the first responders, Dana's head wasn't bleeding massively when they arrived. One paramedic quantified the amount of blood at the scene as "20 drops." So why did Huck describe Dana's bleeding as "massive," if it wasn't?

This is perhaps another "truthful lie." According to Dana's trauma surgeon in the emergency room, there would have been a lot of blood wherever her injury had happened. Immediately after Huck allegedly bludgeoned her, I believe, Dana's head bled profusely for hours. Huck applied pressure to stop the bleeding. Later, he washed the blood from her hair, dried the wound as much as possible, clothed her, and staged her in the yoga room. Yes, Dana's bleeding was truly massive. But by the time Huck called 911, he had it under control. He didn't mention it until late in the call because it was no longer an issue. He had handled it already.

The dispatcher asked, "Is there, do you have a clean, dry cloth or a towel or something you can grab?"

Huck answered, "I can't, I can't leave her alone, so I have a yoga towel around her, but I can't get anything else, um, I can't leave her alone."

Notice his repetition of "I can't." He said it four times. Why can't he leave her alone? Why can't he walk a few feet to the laundry nook, and grab one of the clean towels from on top of the dryer, which can be seen in a police photo? Perhaps he can't do anything the dispatcher suggests because he has painstakingly staged the scene. He doesn't dare mess it up by going through the motions of providing aid.

It's also possible that Huck was not even in the yoga room with Dana at the time of the call. It would be like him, in my opinion, to say, "I can't leave her alone," at precisely a time when he has left her alone.

Huck claimed to "have a yoga towel around her." A yoga towel is something that goes over a yoga mat to absorb perspiration. Yoga towels have roughly the same dimensions as a yoga mat; they're two feet wide, and six feet long. A yoga towel is large enough for Huck to wrap around Dana's head like a turban.

The dispatcher asked, "You don't have anything you can tie like a tourniquet, right?"

This sounded odd to me the first time I heard it, but it makes sense. The dispatcher assumed that the yoga towel was relatively small like a gym towel. She was suggesting, I think, that Huck could use a cord or tourniquet to secure the towel to cover the wound and apply pressure, leaving his hands free.

In response, Huck said: "Uh, no, no, no not around her [unintelligible.]" It's worth noting that, according to police photographs of the scene, there were several items nearby in the yoga room that could have been used as a tourniquet to apply pressure to the wound, such as exercise bands and yoga straps.

The dispatcher tried again: "It's like a yoga towel that's like a hand-towel-sized thing?"

Huck misled her by answering: "Yes."

What was the point of his lying about the size of a yoga towel? Was he really holding a yoga towel to Dana's head, or was he merely pretending that he was providing aid? If there was a yoga towel, where did it go? The first responders didn't report seeing it. When asked by police if they saw blood anywhere in the room other than under the victim's head, they said no. Nor did police find a bloody towel in the house. Huck told police that he had thrown the towel in the trash, and the trash truck had taken it away. The curiously incurious detectives were satisfied with this answer.

Again, try to picture the scene as described by Huck. He has a phone in one hand. He is pressing a hand-towel to the back of Dana's head as he holds her in an upright, seated position as her head bleeds massively. If this were true, he would've had blood on his hands and clothes, but surveillance video shows he didn't.

Another thing that jumps out at me as I listen to the recording, which can't be discerned from reading the transcript, is the fact that Dana's iPad was not audible in the background of this call. Huck told investigators that when he returned from walking the dog, he could hear Dana's iPad playing a yoga video in the yoga room through a closed door. Based on the start time and duration of the yoga video, it would have been playing when Huck called 911. If the video was so loud, and playing in the yoga room with Dana, why can't it be heard in the 911 audio?

Perhaps the iPad was not in the yoga room. Or Huck was not in the yoga room with Dana when he talked to the 911 dispatcher. I believe that both could be true. Alternatively: Huck heard a loud crash, ran into the yoga room, saw his wife bleeding massively, took time to fiddle with the iPad volume control, engaged in some sort of combat with her as he tried to lay her down, and then called 911.

The dispatcher continued to focus on providing aid. She started to offer a suggestion: "OK. Take that, put—"

Huck interrupted: "I'm applying pressure but at some point, I have to unlock the gate."

Suddenly, Huck expressed a hint of urgency. He couldn't spend too much time applying pressure to the wound because he needed to hurry up and unlock the gate. Why was he urgent about unlocking the gate? Perhaps because the next "stage" of Huck's performance would entail convincing the first responders, and he was anxious about this. His mortally wounded wife wasn't an emergency for him but dealing with the paramedics was, perhaps.

The dispatcher understood that Huck wanted to get off the phone. She said: "OK. Just keep an eye on her. Keep your phone with you. If she gets worse before we get there, call back on 911. OK? They're on the way."

Huck said: "Alright. Bye."

The duration of the call was just under two minutes. At the end of the call, the time was approximately 8:53 a.m. According to surveillance video, Huck opened the front gate at 8:56 a.m. First responders arrived at 8:57 a.m. This timeline suggests Huck wasn't urgent about opening the gate, after all. Rather, it's more likely he was urgent about getting off the phone. The dispatcher was asking too many questions. The more he said, the harder it would be for him to keep his story straight.

The first time Huck appears on camera after the 911 call, he opens the exterior door of the yoga room. He moves the wood-framed loveseat away from the door. After he opens the front gate, the camera's view of this part of the patio is blocked. If, as I suspect, Huck had placed Dana's iPad on a table near the loveseat when he returned from walking the dog, opening the gate gives him a chance to grab the iPad off the table and put it in the yoga room before paramedics arrive. In police reports, however, none of the first responders mentioned an iPad.

According to the checklist developed by Adams and Harpster, Huck's 911 call demonstrated several guilty indicators:

- No immediate plea for help for victim
- No immediate assessment of victim
- Extraneous information ("She was doing yoga….")
- No urgency
- Only answers what's asked ("7053.")
- Short answers ("Correct.")
- Self-interruption ("So I'm holding her, um, vertic—not not. She's sitting….")
- Conflicting facts (Huck somehow knows that she was doing a headstand, but he didn't see her. Everything's fine, but "it's a little combative.")

- Awkward phrases ("Bleeding from behind.")

Adams and Harpster refer to such calls as 'dirty' calls. They point out that, "in cases involving callers who display guilty indicators, questionable issues often appear at the crime scene. Thus, a 'dirty' call corresponds to a 'dirty' scene." A 'dirty' scene may include the following problems:

- illogical objects near the victim's body,
- implausible witness statements,
- inconsistencies with timelines, and
- impossibilities regarding the victim's physical condition and location at the scene.

Huck's call to 911 was a dirty call, I believe, and the scene of Dana's death was a dirty scene. Huck's 911 call was not included on the disc of digital media in Bryan's notebook. Rather, I had to wrangle the recording from the Long Beach Fire Department. They initially denied my request for it. It's my impression that police never requested a copy, and probably never listened to it before I posted it online in late June 2014.

From March 2014 through the summer of 2014, my dad's Denver-based lawyers repeatedly asked Detective Johnson to meet with us. Johnson declined, saying he was too busy touring colleges with his son Blake, a top-rated football punter who eventually committed to the Arkansas Razorbacks that summer.

On September 16, 2014, my dad and I at last got a chance to meet with Johnson. He raised an interesting point. When the paramedics found Dana, she was severely injured, but she wasn't dead. If Huck meant to murder her, why did he call 911 to get help for her while she was still alive? The mere fact that Huck called 911 indicated his innocence, didn't it?

No. Huck called 911 to establish his alibi, not to get help for Dana. By that time, she was beyond help.

6. DIRTY SCENE

Huck called my mom in a panic. "Discombobulated," was how she described him. He was sorry to break the news to her, he said. He had tried to call my dad and me, but we weren't answering our phones. He didn't want to be the one to tell her Dana had been seriously injured in a yoga accident. She had fallen somehow. He found her, lifted her head, and saw blood. Dana struggled with him, and suddenly went limp. The paramedics had taken her away. He was overwhelmed. What should he do?

My mom told him to go to the hospital.

Huck said he would drop Enzo at a neighbor's house and take a shower first.

Maybe an hour later, he called me. He still hadn't arrived at the hospital. He told me he had found Dana face-down in a pool of blood in the "yoga room." Huck said he lifted Dana by her hips, turned her over, and she hit him. She told him to leave her alone because she needed to finish her yoga routine. "She's strong like that," he said. "You know how strong she is."

In his varying stories, Huck implied Dana was violent toward him. She was combative, or struggling, or hitting him. In their analysis of 911 homicide calls, Adams and Harpster noted that guilty callers often insulted or blamed the victim. For example, one guilty caller said, "My girlfriend shot herself. The crazy bitch shot herself in the head."

In retrospect, Huck's claims of Dana's "combativeness" strike me as similar. At the time, however, I didn't know what to make of Huck's story. I guessed maybe they'd had a fight and Dana ended up with a bloody nose.

The idea of a "yoga accident" was immediately absurd to me. Sometime in 2012 or 2013, the book *The Science of Yoga: The Risks and the Rewards* by William J. Broad had gotten enough publicity that I had read an article about it. The most serious risks cited by Broad were neck trauma related to doing headstands, and "yoga strokes" in which blood supply to the brain is interrupted, possibly resulting in brain damage. Dana and I talked about this because I knew she could do headstands. She assured me that, over the years, she had gained the flexibility, strength, and awareness to do the pose safely.

After Dana's death, I scoured Broad's book for information about "yoga falls." The most serious example I could find was this:

> "…a male patient fainted while doing yoga in a warm room, falling and hitting his head hard enough to produce a bruise."

My dad had a bad feeling about Huck's descriptions of Dana's alleged accident. Dad was making plans to catch the first available flight from Denver to L.A. He was 86 years old at the time, and in fine condition to travel. Still, I told him I would go instead. He insisted on going, too. That evening, my parents and I landed at LAX. I texted Huck to tell him we had arrived. He replied that Dana had tubes sticking out of her head, and I should prepare my mom. Only then did it dawn on me that something horrible might have happened.

Huck was waiting for us outside the main entrance of St. Mary Medical Center. He seemed giddy. He said Dana was in an induced coma for her protection, so she could heal. We followed Huck into the hospital. He said one of his friends had shown him how to get into the ICU using a door other than the visitor entrance. He demonstrated this for us.

We walked into Dana's hospital room and saw that she hadn't just bumped her head or sustained a concussion. Her brain had been destroyed. She was supine on the bed, surrounded by machines. One machine monitored her intracranial pressure. Another machine inflated her lungs. Tubes protruded from her head and mouth. The moment mom saw Dana, she knew she was gone. Shocked and silent, my parents stood and stared at their dead child.

A nurse named Brandon was in the room. I said something like, "So, she's in an induced coma?"

Brandon looked surprised. "No," he said. "It's much worse than that." Dana had sustained irreversible brain damage, he explained. There was no chance her condition would improve. However, an official declaration of brain death would require several more tests and doctors' signatures. A cerebral perfusion scan was scheduled for the morning.

Huck argued with Brandon: "No, she's in a coma, knocked out on painkillers."

Brandon firmly said, "No, she's not." Huck bickered with him. Huck wasn't in grief or denial. He was trying to gaslight Brandon. I didn't pause to wonder why. I turned my attention to my sister.

Dana was on her deathbed. In the context of this shattering reality, Huck's behavior was unimportant. My parents and I knew he was acting strangely; in our experience, he often acted strangely. We didn't ponder it. Our concern was focused on Dana.

After a while, Huck drove my parents to a hotel to get rooms for us. I stayed with Dana. Her skin was hot to the touch. Her left eyelid was bruised and swollen, as if she'd been punched. I called Stephen, our brother, and told him to catch a flight because it was bad.

Huck brought my parents back to the hospital. We all agreed to meet first thing in the morning to be on hand for Dana's cerebral perfusion test. My brother would be arriving at 7 a.m. Huck offered to pick him up at the airport and bring him to the hospital.

Early the next morning, I contacted Huck to make sure he was awake. He replied that he couldn't go to the airport because he had too many things to do. I picked up Stephen at LAX. He and I met our parents at the hospital. Huck didn't show up. Where was he?

The situation felt intensely real yet oddly dreamlike. I attributed this surreal quality to the fact that we were in shock.

We couldn't think critically or analytically. Only later did I understand that the whole scene of Dana's death was what Adams and Harpster might call a "dirty scene." It was bizarre because it was inherently illogical, implausible, and inconsistent with physical facts.

After Dana's death, one of her friends told me he had talked with a paramedic who had been on scene at Dana's house. Reportedly, this paramedic described the scene as weird, but it was hard to say exactly why or how it was weird. There was nothing obviously wrong, but it felt wrong.

According to a police report, officer Stephan Ritchie spoke to paramedics Jeff Thralls and Keith Dixon on the phone. Ritchie wrote:

> "Thralls said the victim was lying supine in kind of the middle of the floor of a large exercise room. She was at least three feet away from any furniture. There was no yoga mat on the floor of this room. As the victim was being treated, Thralls noticed some blood on the floor below her head. ...Once the victim was removed from the home on a gurney and taken into the Rescue, they noticed the victim's pupils were unequal."

Surveillance videos show a fire engine arriving at Dana's house at timestamp 9:21 a.m., followed by an ambulance at 9:29 a.m. Paramedics wheel Dana through the front gate at 9:40 a.m. We can see that she is strapped to a gurney and appears to be unconscious. Her eyes are closed. She does not move. Paramedics load her into the ambulance at 9:41 a.m.

To me, it's odd that 20 minutes went by and Dana was in the ambulance before any of the half-dozen first responders on scene looked into Dana's eyes and noticed her pupils were unequal. A fixed, dilated pupil, sometimes called a blown pupil, can be a grave sign of severe brain swelling. I would think that, with an unresponsive patient showing signs of head injury, a medic would lift the patient's eyelids and shine a light in her eyes to check pupil constriction.

Ritchie's report continued:

> "Dixon said the husband told them he was in another room of the house and his wife was doing yoga in the exercise room located at the southeast corner of the home. He heard what sounded like a 'thump' and went in to check on his wife. He found her lying on the floor of the exercise room but she wasn't able to answer any of his questions. ...The floor of this room is a dark stained concrete. Dixon said this room has some furniture and 'Hawaiian art objects' but the victim was basically lying in the middle of the room away from any of these items. Dixon said the victim wasn't able to speak with them but did respond to his questions by squeezing his hand. Dixon found a large hematoma on the back of the victim's head (base of skull but in the hair). This hematoma was bleeding and there were drops of blood on the concrete floor below her head. He didn't see blood anywhere else in the room. Due to the victim's vital signs, they realized she needed to be transported to a trauma center. The husband requested his wife be taken to St. Mary Medical Center."

I question whether Dana was able to consciously squeeze anyone's hand. We now know Dana was well into the throes of brain death at the time; any movement or contraction of her muscles would have been involuntary, presumably.

Mostly, I wonder why paramedics didn't notice the severity of Dana's injuries. According to the autopsy report, Dana's occipital scalp was split by an irregular laceration measuring one-and-three-quarter inches long. Her occipital bone, the thickest bone in the skull, was broken, with a fracture measuring four-and-one-half inches long. Dana's brain injuries included acute subdural hematoma, subarachnoid hemorrhage (thick and severe), brain contusions, intracerebral hemorrhage, intraventricular hemorrhage, and transtentorial herniation.

Police photographed the back of Dana's head in the hospital on March 4, 2014. At that time, more than 24 hours after it was inflicted, the deep wound in her scalp continued to ooze blood, despite the presence of nine or more surgical staples.

Clearly, this was not a minor injury that somehow worsened in the hospital, leading to a freak death. This was a massive, mortal wound. Why didn't paramedics notice?

Why, for instance, did they misidentify the deep laceration in Dana's scalp as a superficial hematoma? Typically, a torrent of blood would be flowing from a scalp laceration such as Dana's. Her hair would have been soaked and matted. Later, one of Dana's surgeons told police:

> "Wherever this incident happened, there will be a lot of blood from the laceration on the back of her head."

I'm guessing paramedics were confused by the incongruity of the information presented to them. The lack of blood at the scene combined with Dana's unresponsive state, the placement of her body in the middle of the room with no yoga mat near her, and Huck's story of a yoga fall, all stymied paramedics' ability to read the scene accurately. Something seemed wrong, but it was hard to say exactly what or why. It was a "dirty scene."

At 9:41 a.m., surveillance video from Camera 5 shows Huck raising his cell phone and taking a photo of Dana as she is being wheeled to the ambulance. One of the fire crewmen notices Huck snapping the picture and does a double take. Minutes later, Huck chats on the sidewalk with first responders. While Dana waits in the ambulance, Huck appears to be asking for driving directions. Two of the first responders supportively pat Huck's shoulders.

The ambulance drives away. The fire engine, too, is about to leave. Huck walks through the front gate and into the yoga room. Suddenly, he walks out and shouts at the fire crew. They re-enter the house. Turns out, they had forgotten their EKG machine in the yoga room. Their interaction with Huck is chummy and jocular. One crewman pauses on the sidewalk and chats a bit longer with Huck while the others return to the fire engine. The fire engine drives off camera at 9:45 a.m.

How often do fire crews forget to pack up and take their equipment? To me, this mistake suggests that they weren't thinking procedurally. Because of their chumminess, I wonder whether any of them were friends or acquaintances of Huck or Marian prior to the call that morning.

After the first responders drove away, Huck made phone calls and paced around the house. Enzo remained on the sofa the whole time. The dog didn't leave the sofa even while first responders were there. Earlier, he had followed Huck around eagerly. After the 911 call, however, the dog was subdued, with ears flat and head down most of the time, as if cowering.

At 9:52 a.m., surveillance video from Camera 7 shows something remarkable. As he talks on the phone, Huck pantomimes a "yoga fall." He demonstrates a stance like warrior pose with his legs spread, left foot in front of his right, left knee bent. He takes two steps forward. He stands on his toes and thrusts his head backward. He turns to face the camera. He bends his left arm at the elbow and throws his left hand backward as if imitating the motion of a forceful backward flop. We see him mouth the words, "hit her head."

This is remarkable for a couple of reasons. First, as Huck acts it out, the motion looks biomechanically improbable. Second, his pantomime story contradicts the story he told to the 911 dispatcher less than an hour earlier when he claimed Dana was injured while doing a headstand. This clip of surveillance video plus the 911 recording show that Huck was telling different stories at different times, as if testing to see which tale was most convincing.

A 9:55 a.m., Camera 7 shows Huck at the dining table doing a little sleight of hand. He reaches out with his right hand as if grabbing something off camera. He slides a credit card into his left palm. He turns his back to the camera. He turns again to the table and puts his left hand down. It's empty now. The credit card is gone. He upturns his left palm and, with his right hand, fills it with what appears to be cash or checks. He places the stack of cash on the table and puts Dana's cell phone on top of the stack.

What's the point of this disappearing credit-card trick? Perhaps this was the credit card used in Dana's name to buy a purse online from Levenger.com. Immediately after this "trick," Huck walks down the hallway and returns to the table with a leather-bound, zippered book that I'm pretty sure is his checkbook and wallet.

At 9:58 a.m., Huck again walks down the hallway. He returns to the dining area at 10:05 a.m. His hair looks wet. He has changed his clothes. He is wearing camouflage trousers with a long-sleeved shirt. He packs a bag for himself. He does not appear to pack any items for Dana, such as a book, toothbrush, or her iPad, which has a bright-green case. Instead, he packs other electronic devices and his jacket.

At 10:13 a.m., we see Huck take Dana's purse from the kitchen hutch, remove her wallet from it, and put it in his bag. At 10:15 a.m., he walks out of the house, leaving the front door wide open. The dog seems perplexed by this.

On Camera 2, we see Huck get into Dana's brand-new, white Toyota Prius, which is parked in the driveway. He sits in the car for five minutes. At 10:21 a.m., Huck drives away from the house.

We don't know what time Huck arrived at the hospital. Admission blood samples were drawn from Dana sometime around 9:35 a.m. real time.

According to a police report, officer Stephan Ritchie spoke with ER charge nurse K. Jones who said she had not treated Dana but had seen her when she was admitted to the hospital. The nurse told Ritchie that she didn't recall seeing any visible injuries to Dana's face or body. Ritchie wrote:

> "Given the decedent's inability to talk and her unequal pupils, the ER staff initially thought the decedent suffered a stroke. The doctor ordered a CT scan and the results showed the decedent had a basal skull fracture to the left occipital area, a large occipital hematoma and a large frontal hematoma."

The word "hematoma" in this case refers to brain injuries rather than to Dana's scalp wound.

ER staff also talked with Huck, who claimed Dana had fallen while doing yoga. Ritchie wrote:

> "… ER staff discussed the statement given to them by the husband and what the CT scan results showed and believed it was an 'odd injury for the story'."

Later, a nurse and a doctor told me privately that Huck's affect seemed "off" to them that morning. For example, he talked about getting Dana's will and trust papers together even though hospital staff didn't yet know the extent of her injuries.

The thing that sharpened my suspicion was when Huck missed Dana's cerebral perfusion test on the morning of the 4th. He showed up at the hospital around mid-day saying he had been doing household chores and boarding the dog at a kennel. He had brought along papers regarding Dana's long-term disability insurance to show my dad.

The night before, my dad had asked Huck if Dana had a living will, and whether there were life-insurance policies benefitting Huck in the event of Dana's death. Huck acted as if he didn't know what my dad was talking about. He said the disability policy was the only paperwork he could find.

At some point, Huck had commandeered Dana's e-mail account and sent a message blast to her friends and acquaintances. He told them that she was in an induced coma. Visitors started arriving at the hospital on the 4th. It was nice to see people who cared about Dana, and it was awful to tell them that she was, in fact, brain-dead.

As I stood near Dana's bed, Huck remarked that the situation reminded him of the time she fell in Hawaii. "Remember? She fell and hit her head doing yoga. You were there."

It took me a minute to understand what he was talking about. In May 2009, I was housesitting near Hilo, Hawaii. Dana and Huck came to visit for a week. One morning we went swimming at place we called Pahoa Hot Pond. Its official name is Ahalanui

County Beach Park. It is now permanently closed because it was overrun by lava from a Kilauea volcano eruption in 2018.

In 2009, the park featured a natural thermal pond surrounded by lava rocks. Dana climbed a ladder out of the water and walked a few steps toward her towel. She slipped on the wet rocks. To me it looked as if she was falling in slow motion. She adjusted her posture and landed safely on her butt. She never came close to hitting her head. We joked that Madam Pele, the Hawaiian volcano goddess, had given Dana an "ass tattoo" as a souvenir from the island.

To me, this incident was a perfect demonstration of her fitness and yoga reflexes. It was the exact opposite of how Huck was trying to characterize it.

Later, on March 10, 2014, I explained this to Detective Johnson. Ultimately, Johnson chose to believe Huck's version, and to believe that this alleged "yoga fall" had happened recently rather than five years prior to Dana's death.

Late in the afternoon on March 4, 2014, we got some answers about the nature of Dana's injuries. A nurse practitioner and a social worker led us into a private room. The nurse walked us through images of Dana's skull and brain. There was no sign of a stroke or a previous head injury, she explained. The scans showed Dana had been hit with a heavy blow that fractured her skull. There were two points located an inch or so apart where the impact of the blow appeared to be greatest. Also, doctors had surgically repaired a deep laceration in Dana's scalp. This cut was in the shape of an upside-down letter L.

The social worker asked if we could think of any way in which the injury might have happened. Huck said Dana must've hit her head on the edge of the cabinet in the yoga room. I openly scoffed at this. The surface Huck was describing was approximately three feet off the ground, and Dana was five feet, seven inches tall. Even if her head had hit the edge, it could not have caused the injury described by the nurse.

Huck said maybe Dana had hit her head twice. He acted out a scenario in which Dana struck the back of her head on the cabinet, became disoriented, and slammed her head into the cabinet again, or perhaps threw herself to the floor. It was ludicrous. Huck and I started to argue about it. My brother shushed me because my parents were distraught. My getting into a fight with Huck would compound everyone's misery.

More than a year would go by before I learned that a hospital social worker had called the Long Beach Police Department that afternoon. A recording of her call was included in the notebook. She told the dispatcher:

> "...All the doctors are saying that the nature of the injuries suggests that it may have been foul play. ...They're saying, like, that it sounds like she's doing yoga, and she fell and hit her head, it wouldn't have fractured it that severely."

Doctors thought Dana had been assaulted, she said. She remarked that medical personnel were talking about their suspicions, but no one wanted to call police. She said:

> "And then everyone says it, but nobody wants to call you, so I was like, well, I'm going to call."

Bless her. I'm glad she did. I wonder why no one else would. Why would doctors and nurses hesitate to report a suspected assault and homicide?

According to a police report, officer Christian F. Moody telephoned Dr. Mauricio Heilbron, Jr., a surgeon who had treated Dana in the emergency room. Moody wrote:

> "Dr. Heilbron said Dana Jones arrived at the hospital yesterday morning with a serious head injury. Dr. Heilbron said Dana Jones had a laceration to the back of her head and a blown pupil. Dr. Heilbron said Dana Jones underwent a CT scan which revealed she had bleeding on the front and back of her brain and a skull fracture on the back of her head approximately three inches in length. ...I asked Dr. Heilbron if he believed a person could receive

injuries like Dana Jones from falling while doing yoga. Dr. Heilbron said, 'It could be just a freak accident but in my opinion it looks suspicious. Something could have hit the back of her head causing a lot of trauma. Wherever this incident happened, there will be a lot of blood from the laceration on the back of her head. I have seen trivial injuries turn bad though.'"

To me, this is a clear statement that Dana's injuries were serious upon arrival and, in the surgeon's opinion, were suspicious. However, this same statement was interpreted differently by Detective Johnson and Bryan McMahon. Separately, they told me the doctor's statement confirmed that Dana's injuries were trivial but later turned bad, due to a freak accident.

If this is typical of how police distort the statements of medical professionals, I can understand why a doctor might think twice about calling the cops. Then again, California law requires hospital personnel to report cases of suspected assault to local police immediately by phone and to follow up with a written report no more than two days later. Why, in Dana's case, did hospital personnel hesitate to comply?

The most charitable explanation I can come up with is that everyone except Huck was in a bewildered state of cognitive dissonance. The whole scene was a dirty scene designed to gaslight and flummox everyone involved. First, the 911 dispatcher couldn't get any coherent information out of Huck. Second, the paramedics were misled by Huck and couldn't grasp that Dana had sustained a serious head injury. Third, emergency-room personnel didn't know what to make of Dana's visibly uninjured state until they did a CT scan followed by emergency surgery, only to discover that she was beyond saving. Everyone had been baffled by Huck, by design.

Regardless of real or perceived equivocation in statements made by medical personnel about Dana's injuries, Moody wrote in his report:

"Believing the circumstances surrounding Dana Jones' injuries may be suspicious, I prepared a search warrant for the residence of 7053 Stearns Street, which was signed by Los Angeles Superior Court Judge Meyer. I gave the signed search warrant to Detective T. Johnson, who searched 7053 Stearns Street with Detective R. Zottneck."

Police had probable cause to believe that a felony had been committed. Officers were dispatched to investigate a possible assault with a deadly weapon. In the words of the search warrant, detectives were commanded to search for "any evidence related to the possible crime of murder." There's no ambiguity in the warrant about the nature and purpose of the case. It was a suspected homicide.

With the involvement of homicide detectives and a judge, one might assume that facts would be gathered, alibis would be questioned, claims would be tested, and confusion would be resolved. Sadly, no. Instead, the gaslighting and lies were amplified, augmented, and endorsed under color of law.

7. Under Color of Law

Dana's case was unfolding in a climate of retaliation, intimidation, coverups, and malignant incompetence by public officials backed by public institutions. The story of Judge Judith L. Meyer offers a telling example.

Judge Meyer signed the first search warrant in Dana's case. Later, in 2017, in open court, Judge Meyer criticized Detective Johnson for botching a different murder investigation. At the time, Judge Meyer said the behavior of Long Beach detectives in the case was "appalling and unethical and inappropriate." Her words were quoted in the *Long Beach Press-Telegram* in an article by Jeremiah Dobruck published on April 23, 2018.

This botched murder investigation began in 2010 when Johnson and his partner were assigned to the case of a young man gunned down in the street near his home. Angie Christides, prosecutor from the Los Angeles District Attorney's Office, complained to her supervisors that Johnson and his partner "were involved in a series of either blunders or intentional omissions during the investigation."

Christides reportedly recommended adding Johnson to the "Brady list," a list of police officers whose credibility is subject to court review because they have knowingly lied in an official capacity.

Johnson's superiors defended him, blaming the prosecutor for mistakes in the case. Johnson retaliated against the prosecutor by filing a complaint with the State Bar of California.

Meanwhile, police officers paid a private visit to Judge Meyer. In a secret letter dated the same day the *Press-Telegram* report was published, Judge Meyer recanted her criticism and vouched for the integrity of the detectives.

A report by Dobruck and Kelly Puente published in the *Long Beach Post* on April 18, 2019, quoted one local attorney's reaction to this private visit from police:

"They basically went into the judge's chambers with documents in their hands to try to convince her that she made a mistake, and they did this in order to save their credibility. Why would you do it in this fashion if not to intimidate? This speaks to the level they will go to protect themselves."

A visit from Long Beach police can make even a well-respected superior court judge change her tune. To salvage the credibility of Detective Johnson, top brass went to bat for him, putting the integrity and credibility of the entire police department on the line. These facts illuminate what happened next with Dana's case.

My heartsick parents and I had just left the hospital after the meeting with the social worker and nurse who explained Dana's injuries. We were grappling with the disturbing impression that my sister had died under suspicious circumstances. Huck wanted us to follow him home. He and my brother were ahead of us in Dana's car.

A small army of police officers in front of Dana's house was a welcome sight. Flashing lights lit up the block in red and blue. I thought the good guys had arrived.

Officers asked Huck to remain in the driveway as they waited for the search warrant and homicide detectives Todd Johnson and Roger Zottneck. Huck kept talking about the home's awesome surveillance system and "smart home" electronic features. My brother later told me he thought Huck should keep his mouth shut. If Huck would be arrested, Stephen wanted it to be on suspicion of murder, not because Huck said something insulting to police.

Huck bragged that his cameras recorded everything happening in and around his house. Police became very interested in the surveillance system.

Later, I would write to the Long Beach Citizen Police Complaint Commission:

"Police investigators focused on the cameras to the exclusion of everything else. Police were willfully blind to homicide evidence that was right in front of their eyes."

That night, homicide detectives placed an evidence marker near a pair of shoes Huck had worn. The shoes were in the dining area, next to one of the orange chairs, far from the yoga room. Just inches from the marker, blood evidence is clearly visible. Blood spatter can be seen on a chair leg. A streak of blood runs down the chair back.

Police photos taken in the master bath show a dark trail on the floor running from the bathroom door and into the room. I suspect Dana was in the bathroom when she was bludgeoned in the back of her head. Markings on the concrete floor suggest that, at some point in the attack, Dana's bleeding head was near the bathroom door, and she was dragged toward the shower.

Reddish-brown tread prints from Birkenstock sandals can be seen on the bathroom floor, too. In home-surveillance videos, Huck can be seen wearing Birkenstock sandals prior to changing his clothes and taking the dog for a walk.

The resolution of the police photos is high enough to show no hair on the bathroom floor. Having hair like Dana's, I'm confident that the only time when not a single strand of hair can be found on the bathroom floor is immediately after the floor has been cleaned.

I suspect Huck tried to clean the bloodstains off the floor in the master bath but was unable to remove them completely. To further disguise the bloodstains, he coated the floor with decorative stain. He had applied decorative stain to concrete surfaces throughout the house in the past, as noted in the *This Old House* article about the kitchen remodel.

Despite visible blood in the dining area and suspicious stains in the master bath, homicide detectives failed to test chemically for the presence of blood anywhere in the house that night.

In police photos, more than one dozen dumbbells are clearly visible in the yoga room. Later, it occurred to me that the hexagonal edges of the dumbbells might match what the nurse had told us about Dana's scalp laceration being shaped like an upside-down letter L, accompanied by two points of impact to her skull that were about an inch apart.

Police photos show other possible weapons in the house, such as a dumbbell seemingly out of place near the kitchen hutch, a set of golf clubs in the garage, and a wrist-rocket slingshot with a plastic bag of marbles and metal ball bearings on the floor of the master bedroom next to Huck's nightstand. Police photos also show State Farm life-insurance papers on the dining table.

Police removed the surveillance DVR and Dana's iPad from the house, along with some of Huck's clothes. Notably, the orange t-shirt Huck had worn for much of the morning on March 3 was not obtained by police. We couldn't understand why police didn't take Huck's computer, iPad, and multiple phones, too.

That night, Detective Johnson talked to my dad and brother, assuring them that Huck was totally innocent. Johnson said he had searched the house thoroughly and didn't find anything suspicious. A guy would have to be crazy to kill his wife with so many cameras in his house.

We thought Johnson might be playing a game to make Huck think he had been cleared. We thought, surely, the police would aggressively investigate. We were wrong. Johnson had decided right then and there that Dana had died in a yoga accident.

Later, I spoke to one of Johnson's former partners who told me Johnson had a reputation for reaching hasty conclusions about cases. More experienced investigators like Zottneck were paired with Johnson to make him slow down and do things by the book. Zottneck was weary of this in 2014. He went on leave soon after Dana's death.

Huck wasn't arrested. The next day at the hospital, he seemed ecstatic. He retained all rights as Dana's next of kin. He signed papers authorizing the harvesting of her vital organs for donation. He informed us that Dana would be cremated as soon as possible. He would have her ashes tattooed into his skin. He knew people with cremains tattoos, he told us, and thought it was cool. He planned to mix Dana's leftover ashes with the ashes of her long-dead dog, a Vizsla named Roger.

We thought this plan macabre and insulting to Dana, but we had no legal standing to prevent Huck from doing whatever he wished. We decided to appear to go along with him while trying to talk him out of it. Eventually, my dad struck a bargain by agreeing to pay all mortuary and memorial expenses in exchange for half of Dana's ashes. Even in death, I thought, Huck was holding her hostage, calculating her ransom.

Dana's case had become a coroner's case. Once a hospital patient is declared dead and falls under the coroner's jurisdiction, laws protect the integrity of a homicide investigation. For example, the person's entire body along with his or her clothing, whether removed from or still on the body, becomes evidence belonging to the coroner.

Doctors officially pronounced Dana dead on March 6, 2014. That afternoon, my parents and brother returned to Denver. After they left, Huck left the hospital, too, and, as far as I know, never returned to see Dana. I would stay in Long Beach for as long as Dana was in the hospital, and longer to ensure receipt of half of Dana's ashes from the mortuary. Dana remained in her hospital bed as her organs were tested and prepared for harvesting surgery, which was scheduled for March 8.

During the afternoon on March 6, a nurse came into Dana's room and we briefly talked. She told me a doctor who had treated Dana in the emergency room was nearby in the ICU. I asked her to find out if the doctor would be willing to talk to me. The nurse brought him into the room and closed the door behind her.

The doctor told me Dana's case hit close to home for him. His wife was Dana's age and was a yoga practitioner, too. He was on his way to his son's baseball game shortly after treating Dana when he called police. He spoke to an officer he knew whose name was Moore, I think, but perhaps it was Moody. The officer asked if Dana might have been hit with a baseball bat. The doctor said, yes, her injuries were consistent with being hit with a bat. When the doctor heard organ harvesting had been approved, he knew Huck had gotten away with the perfect crime. In the doctor's experience, organ harvesting would not be allowed unless authorities had decided not to pursue a homicide investigation.

The coroner's office had approved the harvesting of Dana's organs by a company called One Legacy. Later, I learned from a filing in a civil lawsuit that, at the time of Dana's death, the L.A. County Coroner's Office had disturbingly close ties with One Legacy.

A whistleblower retaliation suit filed on May 10, 2017, by coroner investigator Denise Bertone reads in part:

> "One Legacy is a private non-profit organization that is the only organ and tissue harvesting company in Southern California, and has significant influence over the Los Angeles County Coroner's Department.
>
> One Legacy has unfettered access to the Coroner Department's private crypt, which it monitors on a daily basis to examine decedents in order to identify target donors. One Legacy also has complete access to the Department's secure computer system, from which it obtains next of kin contact information to obtain authorization for harvesting. In addition, the Department has an insurance policy, purchased by One Legacy, for legal claims relating to organ and tissue donations.
>
> One Legacy is required to obtain consent from a Coroner Department doctor before it can harvest the decedent's organs or tissue. Certain doctors in the Department never refuse consent, so One Legacy can always obtain consent to harvest if it asks certain doctors in the Department, even in cases where it is critical to preserve the decedents' bodies for homicide investigations."

Bertone's lawsuit stemmed from a troubling incident in 2013 involving the death of a boy. According to the filing:

"Before the boy died, he had entered a coma after being submerged in a washing machine. The boy was then taken to a hospital where One Legacy obtained consent from his guardians to have his organs harvested for donation after his cardiac death. ...While the boy was still alive, he was taken off the ventilator, but then continued to gasp for air, and did not go into cardiac arrest. When the boy failed to go into cardiac arrest, the attending physician administered 500 micrograms of Fentanyl—a strong narcotic—to the boy with the purpose of inducing his death while the harvesting team was waiting in the operating room. After the 500 micrograms of Fentanyl were administered, the boy went into cardiac arrest and died, after which One Legacy harvested his organs."

Bertone contends L.A. County Coroner Dr. Mark Fajardo closed the investigation into the boy's death in October 2013, falsely stating on the death certificate that the boy died due to consequences of "near drowning" rather than fentanyl. Bertone claims Fajardo told her he had no doubt the boy was killed for his organs, but "you just can't say that." Further, Fajardo allegedly warned Bertone:

"While you work for me, you will never criticize One Legacy."

It's a shocking case in which, allegedly, the coroner was willing to overlook homicide for the sake of extracting a child's organs.

I can't help but wonder whether the coroner's office was as forgiving and organ-hungry in Dana's case. Except for her ruined brain, Dana was remarkably healthy. One Legacy took and transplanted her heart, liver, kidneys, lungs, and more. Sick and dying people benefited incalculably from Dana's gifts.

Still, I don't think Fajardo or One Legacy should pat themselves on the back. Considering their cozy, ghoulish relationship, it's likely that the coroner's office prioritized harvesting Dana's organs over seeking justice for her. She was a defenseless victim of crime, and instead of advocating on her behalf, Los Angeles County stripped her for parts. She could not have foreseen this when she opted to be an organ donor on her driver's license.

The day Dana's organs were taken, March 8, 2014, was a Saturday. On Sunday, I called the coroner's office to ask what would happen next. I was worried that Huck, as next of kin, could refuse to let her body be autopsied. The person I talked to assured me the autopsy would happen and suggested I call back on Monday. On Monday, March 10, I was told Dana's body had not been received by the coroner's office. The hospital told me Dana was no longer there. Where was she?

At 11 a.m., I visited the headquarters of the Long Beach Police Department. I asked to speak to the detective in homicide who was handling the case of Dana Jones. The officer at the information window looked up Dana's name in a computer and said there was no record of any case. I told him a dozen or more patrol cars and investigators had spent hours at Dana's house on the night of March 4. Officers had conducted a door-to-door canvas of her street. The officer told me he could find no police record of a call to Dana's address ever. He gave me the phone number for the homicide desk.

I called homicide and spoke to a woman who did not recognize the name Dana Jones. She asked if I meant someone named Perez. I repeated the name Dana Jones. The woman made a sound of recognition and said Detective Johnson would be the person to talk to, but detectives aren't in on Mondays. I left my name and number and told her I wanted to meet with Johnson in person if possible.

Johnson had done nothing to advance the homicide investigation. The reason why no one could find information about Dana's case is because Johnson had decided there was no case. He had dropped it.

Later, I learned that a woman named Kristi Perez had been murdered by her husband, who in turn had killed himself. Johnson and Zottneck had been assigned to the Perez case. This murder-suicide happened on March 6, 2014, two days after Johnson and Zottneck had been assigned to Dana's case.

Worried that Dana's body had gone missing and police couldn't care less, I drove to the coroner's office in Boyle Heights near downtown Los Angeles. The building looked familiar to me from movies and TV. It's a famous brick edifice built in 1909 known as the "Old Administration Building." To me, it looked like a haunted building in a scary part of town. At 1:15 p.m., I inquired at the information desk about the location of my dead sister's remains.

Dana's body was not in the possession of the coroner's office at that time, I was told, and no investigator had been assigned to her case. I asked to be notified when an investigator was assigned.

I stayed off the freeway as I drove slowly back to Long Beach. I was glad to sit in traffic because it seemed to be the only normal thing. I couldn't understand why no one cared about Dana. No one was even mildly curious. It was as if women died of alleged yoga-induced head trauma every minute of every day.

At 1:58 p.m., Detective Johnson called me. I pulled into a parking lot. We spoke for 25 minutes and 46 seconds.

Johnson told me he had seen surveillance video from Dana's house. It backed up Huck's story, he claimed. No further investigation was pursued.

I argued with Johnson. I told him that if he looked, he would find a mountain of incriminating evidence. I knew this because I knew Huck.

Johnson claimed that too much time had passed for police to go back to the scene and look for things they had missed. He said Huck already had too much time to think up answers to possible police questions. Johnson said he could not question Huck any further because he would "lawyer up." The only way he could make an arrest, he said, was if Huck came in and confessed.

Johnson said Dana had a previous head injury from a yoga fall in Hawaii. Huck had told him all about it. I explained that it wasn't a yoga fall, Dana hadn't hit her head, and she hadn't been to Hawaii in years. Johnson dismissed everything I said. He sounded amused, as if it was a game, as if it was hilarious that I was upset. I kept saying, "Oh my God." Oh my God, Huck was getting away with murder.

That night, I typed up my notes about the conversation and e-mailed them to my dad's lawyer in Denver. The next day, I cut-and-pasted most of these notes into an official complaint addressed to the Long Beach Citizen Police Complaint Commission.

A few hours after we spoke on the phone, Johnson filed his first report about Dana's case. Six days had passed since he had searched Dana's house. The report is brief, fewer than 400 words. I will quote it all.

On March 10, 2014, at 4:32 p.m., Johnson wrote:

> "On March 4, 2014, I (Detective Johnson) was contacted by Sergeant Richens regarding a suspicious accidental fall of a female, later identified as Dana Jones that occurred on March 3, 2014, at approximately 0945 hours at 7053 Stearns Street. Sergeant Richens further advised that Jones is on a ventilator and has no brain activity and the family plans to harvest the body."

It's telling that Johnson mischaracterizes the nature of the investigation from the outset as a "suspicious accidental fall." Other police reports filed prior to Johnson's characterize the case as a possible assault with a deadly weapon. Even the police photos begin with a title card reading in part, "poss 187 pc," or "possible homicide," referencing the statute number pertaining to homicide in the California penal code.

Why did Johnson deceptively mischaracterize the nature of the case in his report?

Notice, too, Johnson's claim that Richens told him "the family plans to harvest the body." On March 3 and 4, we knew nothing about plans to "harvest the body." Not even Huck mentioned it. During this time, doctors were still running tests to confirm brain death before Dana could be declared dead. It wasn't until March

5, the day after Johnson proclaimed Huck totally innocent, that my parents, brother, and I heard anything about organ donation. None of the other officers mentioned organ donation in their reports, not Richens, and not Moody, who had interviewed hospital personnel.

Johnson wrote in his report:

> "Jones was doing Yoga in the northeast bedroom when her husband Cain Finn Jones heard a crash."

Johnson states this as if it's true. It's the story Huck told. Without testing or questioning it, Johnson endorses Huck's dubious claim as fact.

I should explain that "Cain Finn Jones" is one of Huck's names. When they were married, Huck's name was Carl Lynn Jenkins. After his stepfather Rusty Jenkins died, Huck changed his name to Cain Finn Jones in 2010. At the time, Dana and Huck had been married for 10 years. He was a middle-aged man. We thought it odd that Huck suddenly insisted on taking the surname Jones. Dana bristled at the name Cain. She told Huck it was an unfortunate choice for a contractor because, in the Bible, Cain was a murderer who died when the house he had built for himself collapsed on him. Five months after Dana's death, Huck changed his name to Kane Finn Kealoha. Detective Johnson apparently found nothing suspicious about these name changes.

In his report, Johnson wrote regarding Huck:

> "He checked the surrounding yards thinking the crash sound came from outside. He eventually went into the room where his wife was doing Yoga and found her on her back on the concrete floor. He put his hand behind her head and felt blood. He called for Long Beach Fire. They arrived and treated her injury and transported her to St. Mary's Hospital."

When I talked to him on the phone, Johnson told me he had studied the surveillance video. But if he had, he would have known Huck didn't "check the surrounding yards." The video shows nothing of the kind. I question whether Johnson had seen any of the surveillance video at the time he wrote this report.

Johnson's report continues:

> "My partner (Detective Zottneck) and I drove to St. Mary's Hospital and responded to the Intensive Care Unit (ICU) and located Dana Jones in Pod 5 Room 3. Jones was supine in a hospital bed on her back with her head facing west. She was attached to a ventilator and monitoring devices."

Johnson makes it sound as if Sergeant Richens contacted him about a "suspicious accidental fall," he and Zottneck hopped in the car, drove to the hospital, and found a brain-dead woman awaiting organ harvesting. End of investigation.

Johnson writes:

> "Due to Jones' brain swelling, an emergency craniotomy was performed on her head to relieve pressure. St. Mary's nurses rolled Jones so we could see her head injury on the back of her head. I noticed a 3 inch cut to the back of her head that had 3 to 4 staples closing the wound."

Accurately recording verified facts about the case wasn't Johnson's aim, it seems. If it had been, Johnson might have taken the trouble to glance at police photos and count at least nine staples closing Dana's wound, for example.

Johnson writes:

> "Dr. Heibron Jr. described the wound on the back of Jones' head, fracture to the left occipital area of the skull and laceration to the lower occipital frontal Hemotoma. The ICU nurse advised us that Jones was given a brain stimulation test and it showed no brain activity."

Did Johnson intend for his description of Dana's injuries to be incomprehensible? In Officer Moody's report, Dr. Heilbron's statement is much clearer.

Johnson's report makes no mention of the suspicions of hospital personnel regarding Dana's injuries. He neglects to mention that police had obtained a search warrant on March 4.

Johnson says nothing about searching Dana's house and seizing evidence. He omits these key facts. What is the purpose of this report?

It's hard for me to believe this line appears in Johnson's report, but it does:

> "The family of Jones plans to donate Jones' organs to 'One Legacy' (A Donate Life Organization) once she is pronounced."

Johnson specifically mentions One Legacy and cites their marketing slogan to boot. It's weird. It's as weird as a police report stating something like, "The decedent was wearing Nike (Just Do It) shoes at McDonald's (I'm Lovin' It) when shot with a Winchester rifle (Gun that Won the West)." It's what Adams and Harpster might call extraneous information. It's an example of repetition, too. Twice now, Johnson has mentioned organ harvesting.

In such a brief report, why did Johnson repeat specific details about something completely unrelated to the question of whether homicide had occurred?

Johnson concludes his report:

> "We asked the ICU staff to notify us when Jones is pronounced because this a coroner's case. On March 6, 2014 at 1035 hours, Dr. Mohsen Rofoogaran pronounced Jones. On March 9, 2014, Jones' organs in her body were harvested by Legacy One and the body was later transported to Los Angeles County Coroner's Office. The Los Angeles County Coroner's Office assigned Coroner's Case #2014-01724."

For the third time, Johnson mentions the harvesting of Dana's organs. In the space of fewer than 400 words, the word "homicide" appears nowhere. "Investigate," "assault," and "question" appear nowhere. The only time anyone is "asked" anything is when the ICU is asked to tell Johnson when Dana is declared dead. The phrase "suspicious accidental fall" appears once. What's suspicious about it? Johnson doesn't say. The word "yoga" appears twice.

By contrast, the words "harvest" and "harvested" appear once each. "One Legacy" and "Legacy One" appear once each. "Donate" appears twice. "Organs" appears twice. He refers to organ harvesting in three places in his brief report, at the beginning, middle, and end.

Johnson's word choices suggest that the point and purpose of this report was not to document facts related to a homicide inquiry. Rather, the emphasis of his report is on the harvesting of Dana's organs by One Legacy.

Why did Detective Johnson focus on this?

Perhaps because he had fumbled badly. Whether due to laziness, intoxication, incompetence, malice, or intentional calculation, Johnson had botched the case. It was too late to preserve Dana's body as evidence in a homicide investigation. Johnson was personally and professionally invested, now, in portraying Dana's death as a tragic accident. In this, Johnson and Huck had joined common cause.

The only public official who would be looking over Johnson's shoulder outside the LBPD was the coroner. With this report, Johnson sent a loud-and-clear message to Dr. Mark Fajardo and the coroner's office. Perhaps Johnson knew of the 2013 case in which a boy was injected with fentanyl to expedite organ procurement. Perhaps Johnson knew the coroner's office was inclined to regard homicide as pardonable if healthy, fresh organs were obtained as a result by One Legacy.

The next day, on March 11, 2014, I emailed my complaint about Detective Johnson to Anitra Dempsey, the executive director of the Long Beach Citizen Police Complaint Commission (CPCC). The next morning, police reports show a sudden flurry of activity regarding Dana's case.

In a report dated March 12, 2014, Detective Zottneck logged the receipt of Dana's iPad and the DVR under tag number 806416. Why were the devices suddenly being logged eight days after they had been taken from Dana's home? The timing of Zottneck's report suggests that, prior to March 12, police had done nothing to analyze the devices. Had they even watched any of the video?

Within an hour of the devices being logged, Forensics Specialist Carmen Moncure logged two swabs into evidence, eight days after they had been collected.

That same morning, Detective Johnson reported picking up tubes of Dana's blood from the hospital. According to the paper trail, Detective Mike Dugan transferred Dana's blood to the sheriff's department crime lab for toxicology analysis. Sergeant Erik Herzog signed off on this transfer. Subsequent documents show that toxicology analysis was not included in Dana's autopsy report. Toxicology screening was not even requested.

Curiously, months later in December 2014, Long Beach Detective Shea Robertson reported taking these same tubes of blood from the LBPD property section with no word about how they had traveled from the sheriff's crime lab back to the LBPD. Months after Dana's body had been cremated, Detective Robertson reported that he gave Dana's blood to the coroner's office. Why? His report doesn't say.

These police reports cast serious doubt on whether the LBPD handled evidence promptly and competently in my sister's case.

I received a letter dated July 9, 2014, from Anitra Dempsey informing me that she had withheld my complaint about Detective Johnson from consideration by the Long Beach Citizen Police Complaint Commission. She wrote:

> "It has been determined by the Police Department's review staff and the CPCC staff that no further action will be taken on your complaint because the allegation that officers failed to conduct an investigation was either disproved by independent witnesses or physical evidence."

A botched investigation still counts as an investigation, it seems. In Long Beach, no one holds police accountable for botched investigations. Not the police department's review staff. Not the CPCC. Not the district attorney. Not the coroner. Not even a judge.

The state attorney general's office doesn't get involved in this kind of thing, either, as they helpfully informed me. In a letter dated May 8, 2019, Casey Hallinan wrote on behalf of Xavier Becerra and the State of California Department of Justice:

> "We suggest that you continue to address your concerns directly to the Long Beach Police Department."

In other words, Detective Johnson and his staunch defenders who are willing to lean on judges and prosecutors when necessary to protect police credibility are the arbiters of justice for Dana.

8. FOUL IS FAIR

As I waited to find out where Dana's body had gone, I thought about my conversation with Detective Johnson. If he had made up his mind about the case, why argue with me for 25 minutes? It would've been easier for him to say he couldn't talk about it, thanks for inquiring, goodbye. I tried to convince myself police were busy combing through evidence. My parents encouraged me to hide my suspicions, be nice to Huck, and reassure him. It was just a matter of time, we naïvely hoped, before he would be arrested.

The afternoon of Wednesday March 12, Coroner Investigator Sherwood Dixson called me to say he had been assigned to Dana's case. He asked me to let the mortuary handle all contacts with the coroner's office.

I texted Huck to find out which mortuary he had chosen. He didn't know he needed to find a mortuary. He felt abandoned, he said. I assured him I would help make the arrangements.

The next day, I sat with him at All Souls. The funeral planner, a woman named Courtney, filled out paperwork. Huck knew hardly anything about Dana. He drew a blank on city of birth, mother's maiden name, date of marriage, and other basic information. I was happy to supply answers because each one was a rebuke to his devoted husband pose.

Courtney left the room to call the coroner. She was gone for what felt like an hour. During this time, Huck talked. He said something about Dana forcing him to sell his dead mother's house in Menifee. Something about my own mother pretending to have sympathy for the pain he still carries from his acne-scarred teen years, but not really caring about him. Something about having spent tens of thousands of dollars on the enclosed front patio, yoga-room remodel, and surveillance cameras. In his mind, Dana had cost him a lot of money over the years somehow.

Enduring the creepiness was worth it to see the look on Huck's face when Courtney returned. Dana's body was ready to be released by the coroner, she said. However, the death investigation would continue for another month. Huck covered his face with his hands and groaned. He pretended to be yawning. I still had doubts about his guilt until I saw him in that moment of fear.

Our appointment at the mortuary ended by mid-afternoon. Huck said he was going to a therapy appointment. I went back to my hotel. I had a room with a view of the Catalina Express terminal. Each day, I watched boats in the channel coming and going from downtown Long Beach to Avalon.

All I knew about Catalina Island was that film star Natalie Wood had drowned off the coast after falling from a boat on a November night in 1981. The coroner's office ruled it an accident. I was 16 years old when her death was in the news, and Dana was 18. We were far away in Colorado, singing along to *California Dreamin'*: "I'd be safe and warm if I was in L.A."

On the evening of March 13, an agitated Huck called my dad. Detective Johnson had contacted him and told him not to freak out. Police were doing another search. My dad insincerely told Huck not to worry.

Huck need not have worried. When I heard police had obtained a second search warrant, I presumed it was because the medical examiner saw foul play and belatedly launched a homicide investigation. Later, I realized the purpose of the second search was to help Johnson cover up his previous mistakes.

Medical examiner Dr. Ogbonna Chinwah concluded that Dana had died of accidental blunt-force head trauma. Dr. Chinwah wrote this description of Dana's injury:

> "On the back of the head 5 inches below the buttocks and located in the midline is an irregular laceration measuring 1-3/4 inches...."

Five inches below the buttocks? If this is a typo, it's a whopper. At best, it's obviously incorrect, and makes it hard to understand precisely where the laceration was located.

Dana's autopsy report included a report by forensic neuropathology consultant Dr. Cho Lwin, who examined Dana's brain. Lwin wrote:

> "The following information is taken from the investigator's summary of the case and Dr. Chinwah's autopsy report. The 50 years old Caucasian female fell to the floor and sustained blunt force head trauma while doing yoga exercises at her residence. CT scan of head revealed skull fracture and subdural hemorrhage. She died 3 days later."

Huck's claim that Dana fell while doing yoga was endorsed by Detective Johnson and repeated in Dr. Lwin's report. It's not Lwin's job to investigate the circumstances. It's disturbing to me that the doctor was given misleading information. Also, Lwin was told Dana "died three days later," when in fact she was observed to be brain-dead on the day she was admitted to the hospital.

Later, Emma R. Hall, the coroner of Boulder County, Colorado, read Dana's autopsy report and talked to me about it over the phone. I thought if anyone else had ever heard of a yoga fatality, it would be Hall, considering the popularity of yoga in Boulder. While the Los Angeles coroner didn't want to hear from me and didn't respond to my subsequent email queries, Hall acted as if explaining autopsy reports to family members of the deceased was part of her public duty.

Hall would not comment on the findings in Dana's case except to say it was a remarkably severe head injury. She had never heard of anything similar inflicted by yoga.

Hall said the neuropathologist's report suggested extra time and expense had been allocated to Dana's case. Dr. Lwin's report made it clear that Dana had not suffered a stroke. Also, the report showed Dana had no pre-existing head injury.

These two points were important because they contradicted the claim that a previous fall had caused a "fatal fall." Coroner investigator Dixson wrote in his report:

> "The decedent experienced a falling episode one year ago while in Hawaii. She reportedly fell and struck the back of her head. She was evaluated and was reported to be fine. During the past three months, the decedent was reported to be moving in slow manner while having difficulty getting up in the morning."

Dixson's statement was the only rationale offered in the autopsy report about why the medical examiner decided Dana's death was an accident.

Over the Thanksgiving holiday prior to her death, my brother and his family had stayed at Dana's house. Stephen told me that, more than once, Huck claimed Dana was acting spacey, confused, or off-balance. Stephen said he dismissed Huck's comments because it was clear to him Huck was wrong. Even then, Huck was laying the groundwork for his alibi, hinting that Dana had a neurological problem. Dr. Lwin's findings showed Huck's claim to be baseless.

The second search warrant, written by Johnson, repeated many of Huck's lies as facts. For instance, Johnson took for granted that Dana was alive and well on the morning of March 3, using her iPad, and doing yoga. However, Johnson also wrote:

> "Detectives viewed the video on the recorder (DVR) from the residence and there is an approximate 8 minute time period that does not match what Victim Jones' husband told Detectives what he did after he heard the crash (noise of something falling)."

This shows that, after watching the video, detectives were aware of discrepancies and inconsistencies in Huck's version of events. They knew his version was unreliable. They chose to rely on it anyway.

According to the warrant, detectives supposedly wanted to search for an "item" in the yoga room that could have caused the "kind of injury" that killed Dana. Johnson failed to mention dumbbells, golf clubs, construction tools, a slingshot, and other possible deadly weapons he had seen and photographed in the house on March 4.

Did Johnson truly believe the weapon would be in the yoga room 10 days after the fact, and nowhere else? Probably not, but detectives weren't necessarily looking for evidence of foul play. Rather, I think they hoped to find *no evidence* of foul play. Johnson restricted the search to the yoga room because, I think, the goal was to find nothing.

Johnson called in the Scientific Services Bureau of the Los Angeles County Sheriff's Department to assist with this search. In a report filed four months after the fact on July 15, 2014, Senior Criminalist Gregory Hadinoto wrote:

> "On March 13, 2014, at the request of Detective Johnson of the Long Beach Police Department, a Field Investigation was conducted at 7053 Stearns Street, in the city of Long Beach. The purpose of the investigation was to process the house for possible biological evidence. Forensic Identification Specialist Martin Mutoc from the Latent Print Section was present for photography purposes. Senior Criminalist Betty Ring from the Biology Section was present for training purposes."

Why were these people called in on March 13 but not on March 4? Why did Johnson let more than a week pass before he saw fit "to process the house for possible biological evidence" such as blood? And why did it take four months for Hadinoto to file a report about it? Hadinoto's report states:

> "The exercise room was tested with the luminol reagent. Four dumbells, one drawer on the hutch, four areas on the floor and one of the black mats luminesced. These areas were tested with a presumptive chemical test for blood and all gave a negative result. No evidence items were collected."

Hadinoto's report doesn't mention any place in the house other than the yoga room. Did they search for blood in the dining area? On the dining chairs? In the master bath? Apparently not. This suggests they weren't searching for blood throughout the house. Rather, they focused on the yoga room and found no blood.

Later, Bryan would tell me no blood was found in the yoga room because Dana's head wasn't bleeding, because her injury wasn't serious until it suddenly turned serious at the hospital. This explained why Huck didn't rush to the hospital. He and paramedics knew Dana's condition wasn't bad; it was just a harmless, superficial hematoma, after all.

The effect of Hadinoto's report, it seems, was to minimize Dana's injury, defend Huck, cover paramedics, and back up Johnson's decision to drop the case.

After the second search, in a report dated March 17, Detective Zottneck wrote that he had taken Dana's iPad and DVR and "released them to the Long Beach Police Department's Computer Crimes section to download." Zottneck doesn't say when this happened. He logged the devices on March 12 under tag number 806416. On March 31 he logged the devices again under different tag numbers—807651 for the DVR, and 807670 for the iPad.

Judging from Zottneck's reports, the devices probably were examined sometime between March 12 and March 31. This was after Johnson had decided to drop the case, and after Dana's organs had been taken. By the time they got around to analyzing the devices, detectives perhaps were more invested in supporting the conclusions they had already reached rather than honestly evaluating the evidence.

After the second search, Zottneck wrote:

> "…detectives contacted Cain Jones who was waiting at Marian Veargin's [sic] house at 7041 Stearns Street. Jones stated he had the workout clothing in his Toyota Prius that Dana Jones was wearing when she was transported to St. Mary's Hospital by Long Beach Fire. I collected the

clothing, which was in a clear plastic bag, from the vehicle and transported it to the Long Beach Police Department's Main Headquarters. I maintained possession of the item until placing it into Police evidence."

This is a telling example of how detectives uncritically accepted evidence from Huck. Zottneck doesn't question whether these really are the clothes Dana was wearing, or why Huck volunteers to give them to police. The first search warrant had commanded detectives to search for "any evidence of the possible crime of murder," specifically mentioning Dana's Prius and her clothes. Why did detectives fail to find this bag of clothes at that time? Zottneck's unquestioning acceptance of these clothes from Huck shows how willing detectives were to be spoon fed.

Zottneck said Huck was waiting at Marian's house while detectives conducted the second search. Surveillance video showed Marian's car parked in front of Huck's house for much of the morning on March 3. She drove away just minutes before he left to walk the dog. Huck told police Marian had helped him clean up Dana's blood. Apparently, none of these facts made detectives curious about the relationship between Huck and Marian.

Officer Keith Mortensen took a statement from Marian on the night of March 4. Mortensen wrote:

> "I, Officer K. Mortensen #5290, working Unit 2C15 in a marked black and white vehicle assisted 2S20, Sergeant M. Richens #6056 at 7053 Stearns Street regarding an Assault with a Deadly Weapon report call."

Notice Mortensen was on "an Assault with a Deadly Weapon report call," rather than a "suspicious accidental fall" case, as Johnson had mischaracterized it. Mortensen wrote:

> "Upon arrival, I talked with a neighbor located at 7041 Stearns Street, who Cain Jones identified as a friend who helped him clean the room where the incident had occurred. I talked with Veargin [sic] who stated she has

known both Dana and Cain for approximately 12 yrs and she has a very close relationship with both."

In fact, Marian once hired Dana to draw plans for her bathroom remodel, but Dana and Marian were not close. Dana considered Marian to be Huck's friend, not hers. She told me Huck and Marian bonded by smoking marijuana together, and Dana wasn't interested in participating.

Mortensen wrote:

> "Veargin [sic] stated she arrived home on 03/03/14 at approximately 1530 hrs, and was told by a neighbor that Dana was in the hospital. She called Cain, she refers to him as 'Huck' and then drove directly to St. Mary's Hospital and arrived there at approximately 1630 hrs. Veargin [sic] left the hospital and drove home at about 2030 hrs."

According to a different police report, two neighbors said they talked to Marian that day, and had a different story about who had told whom Dana was in the hospital. Regarding one of the neighbors, Officer Tina Icorn wrote:

> "He was standing in his front yard with [his housemate] yesterday around 1700 when his neighbor, Mirian [sic] (at 7041 Stearns) pulled her vehicle alongside the curb and told them she had just checked her messages and found Hawk [sic] had called saying Dana had fallen and was in the hospital. When she returned around 2100 hours, she told him she thinks Dana will die. Dana had hit her head doing yoga and slipped or blacked out. She hit her head on something."

Marian was telling neighbors that Dana was in the hospital and repeating the story Huck wanted everyone to believe: Dana had hit her head while doing yoga.

Mortensen wrote:

> "The next morning Veargin [sic] could not remember if she called Huck or if he called her. She asked him if he needed anything and he asked her if she could go with him

to walk the dog. She agreed and they walked to the park with the dog. After the walk, she asked Huck if he needed help with anything else and he asked her if she would help him clean the room where the incident happened and she agreed."

Mortensen conducted this interview on the night of March 4 as detectives searched Huck's house for the first time. Marian told Mortensen about events that supposedly happened earlier in the day, and yet she claims she can't remember who called whom. This was also the morning of Dana's cerebral perfusion test, when Huck was supposed to pick up Stephen at the airport and bring him to the hospital. I picked up my brother instead. Huck didn't show up at the hospital until around noon. Mortensen wrote:

> "Veargin [sic] stated that she had been an ER nurse for 25 years and that the sight of blood does not bother her. Veargin [sic] said she was in the house and saw that the door to the Yoga room was closed. She said this was normal in order to keep the dog out of the room. She entered the room and saw that there was a blue yoga mat and a white towel on the ground. She believes there was a couple drops of blood on the yoga mat and stated that she wasn't paying attention to the towel, so she does not remember if there was any on it."

The paramedics who were interviewed by police said there was no blood anywhere in the room on March 3 except under Dana's head. One paramedic estimated the amount of blood to be "20 drops." Notably, both paramedics said there was no yoga mat in the room.

In his 911 call, Huck described Dana's bleeding as "massive." He said he was applying pressure with a hand-towel-sized "yoga towel." Are Marian and Huck talking about the same towel? If so, why *wouldn't* it have blood on it? If there was a bloody towel in the room, why didn't paramedics notice it? Mortensen wrote:

> "I asked how much blood was on the ground and she stated that she was not paying attention to it and just

helped clean it. I asked if the blood was already dry and she stated that it was. Veargin [sic] said that she stayed with Huck the entire time, and she believes that he made a concentrate of warm water, simple green and bleach. He placed this into a bucket and she thinks she used a sponge to clean it up the blood. Yeargin said that Huck helped and he used a brush of some kind."

Why were a bucket of solvent, a sponge, and a brush necessary to clean mere drops of dried blood?

Marian also says she "stayed with Huck the entire time," as if recalling a significant amount of time. I wonder why she felt the need to say this.

I get the impression that early in the morning on March 3, Marian ran an errand and returned to Huck's house. Video shows her parking at the curb just before 7 a.m. Saying that she had "stayed with Huck the entire time" during the blood cleanup seems to anticipate a question. Mortensen couldn't possibly have known to ask: Did you run to a 24-hour pharmacy to buy a wound-sealing product or any other product that might've helped you, an experienced trauma nurse, to conceal or disguise the nature of Dana's injuries? Did you leave the house to dispose of bloody items?

Prior to studying the surveillance video, police could not have guessed that Marian was in Dana's house early in the morning on March 3, left, returned, and left again before Huck walked the dog, but I think it's likely. Therefore, to me it sounds as if Marian is preemptively answering an unasked question when she states that "she stayed with Huck the entire time."

Mortensen wrote:

> "I again asked her how much blood was on the ground and asked her to show me using her hands, and she stated that she really couldn't say."

Marian described herself as an ER nurse with 25 years of experience, and yet she "really couldn't say" how much blood she saw. In my experience, nurses are skilled at estimating quantities of fluid in terms of cubic centimeters. I'm guessing Marian had cleaned up more than a pint of Dana's blood on March 2 and 3 before paramedics arrived at the house. Perhaps this was something she "really couldn't say" to police, so she equivocated about the amount of blood. Mortensen wrote:

> "After cleaning the blood she brought the trash cans to the front of the backyard and Huck threw the towel and yoga mat away."

That day was trash day in Huck and Marian's neighborhood. The City of Long Beach advises residents to put their bins at the curb by 6 a.m. for trash pickup. Marian said she "brought the trash cans to the front of the backyard" so Huck could throw away a towel and a yoga mat. Presumably, Huck's bins were at the front curb awaiting pickup. Wouldn't it have been easier to carry the mat and towel to the curb? Also, why were trash *cans*, plural, necessary?

Based on Marian's statement, it sounds as if she was equipped to clean a lot of blood, and that the task took an "entire" time. It sounds as if the disposal of waste was facilitated by moving trash cans in the backyard. To me, this suggests a bigger cleanup job than wiping 20 drops of dried blood off a floor.

Marian tells Mortensen this cleanup effort happened that morning, on Tuesday, March 4. If detectives had preserved all video on the DVR from Huck's house, they might have been able to fact-check this claim.

Huck's description of the cleanup differed from Marian's. Officer Edwin Oak wrote:

> "Marian Yeargin, who lives a couple houses down came over and asked Jones if she could help him with anything. He asked her if she would take a walk with him and they took a long walk around the neighborhood. When they returned to his residence, he asked her if she would help clean up the blood in the recreation room. Since Yeargin use to be a nurse, he said the site of blood did not offend her. Jones could not bare seeing the blood and being

reminded of his wife lying there on the ground. Jones and Yeargin went in and washed the dried blood away. Yeargin began to scrub very hard and began to remove the black stain that was on the concrete. This caused a brownish/yellowish color to appear and Jones stopped Yeargin from scrubbing any more. There on the ground, he saw a circle on the concrete where the black stain was scrubbed off and it was a constant reminder to him of where her head was lying when he entered into the room.

Jones stated the cleanup took only a few minutes and he threw away the towels they used to clean up the blood, along with the yoga mat that was in the room. He placed a candleholder where her head was and lit several candles. The trash was picked up that day so the yoga mat and t-shirt used to clean the floor were no longer in his possession."

According to Huck, Marian obsessively scrubbed that "damned spot" so hard she stripped decorative stain off the floor. Thinking back to the surveillance video and Huck's repeated scrubbing and wiping of the kitchen counters, I suspect that if anyone was scrubbing, it was him.

Huck says they threw away towels—plural—and a yoga mat. Out of nowhere, Huck also mentions a t-shirt used to clean up blood. Whose t-shirt? Why?

Four different people—Huck, Marian, and two paramedics—told police about the presence of blood in the yoga room. Huck and Marian described blood-cleanup efforts that did not seem to match the amount of blood that paramedics had described very specifically in terms of drops.

If Huck and Marian had cleaned up a lot of blood, did this cleanup happen on March 2 and 3 before Huck called 911?

Days later, Johnson and Hadinoto got around to searching for blood, found none in the yoga room, and stopped looking. In the dining room, blood was visible to the naked eye but went unnoticed by multiple investigators. Stains on the master bathroom floor, too, were not noted.

Medical examiners Chinwah and Lwin were given misleading information about the circumstances of Dana's injury, such as the claim that she had fallen previously, and was in the hospital for three days before she died. Later, local news media reported that under the leadership of Dr. Mark Fajardo, the L.A. County Coroner's Office was in disarray with a backlog of more than 400 cases. After two years on the job, Fajardo resigned the post.

Considering police lapses and chaos in the coroner's office, how can my family and I have confidence in the conclusions reached by law enforcement and the medical examiner?

People tell me the coroner's office almost never changes a ruling. It has happened in the past, but rarely. One such case was the death of film star Natalie Wood. In January 2013, the coroner revised the ruling on manner of death, saying her drowning was due to undetermined factors rather than an accident. This change came after the L.A. Sheriff's Department reopened the investigation in 2011.

It took 30 years of celebrity allure, ongoing speculation, and enduring suspicion before law enforcement took a fresh look at the Natalie Wood case. It took more than 30 years for the coroner to acknowledge evidence of assault found on Wood's body. Even then, the manner of her death was ruled undetermined rather than homicide.

Some people in Los Angeles question whether revisiting the Wood case merited the expenditure of public resources. No one was punished in the matter. Why bother?

I've been asked similar questions. People say, OK, maybe the police messed up and Huck got away with murder. So what? Punishing him won't change anything. Maybe the coroner messed up, too. But Dana's vital organs saved other people's lives, which is great. And maybe it was a terrible yoga accident after all. Poor Huck.

Why can't you drop this case, Lisa? Everyone else can. What's wrong with you?

9. UNRESOLVED

On the morning of March 3, 2019, exactly five years after Dana was wheeled from her house on a gurney, armored vehicles and FBI agents swarmed her neighborhood. They weren't breaking down Huck's door, however. They were a mere 175 yards southeast of Huck's house breaking down the door of his neighbor Stephen Beal.

Months earlier, Beal had been investigated in connection with a package-bomb explosion that had killed Beal's ex-girlfriend, a spa owner named Ildiko Krajnyak. Beal was arrested briefly and released because the FBI didn't have enough evidence to charge him with a crime.

Beal's neighbors were eager to vouch for his innocence and good character. "We can't fathom he would do anything mean, or nasty, or anything else," one neighbor told the press.

Beal was said to be a model-rocket enthusiast who made small explosives to help a neighbor with a "gopher problem." Another neighbor told a reporter:

> "Everyone can see how he was a suspect because of the relationship, but they couldn't find anything. They gathered the evidence, and the system worked, and there was nothing that could tie him to the explosion. We're just glad he's free to have his life back."

Another neighbor was quoted as saying: "I feel sorry for him. You can be able to build rockets and not be able to build a bomb that'll blow up in a box."

Beal was later arrested again by federal agents and charged with "use of a weapon of mass destruction resulting in death," among other things. He pleaded not guilty. I don't know if his neighbors still vouch for his innocence.

I mention these expressions of support and sympathy for Beal because I heard neighbors say similar things about Huck. On the night of March 4, 2014, Dana's neighbors talked to one another, and to me and my family, as police conducted the first search. One woman told me she was shocked that Huck's privacy was being invaded. Her husband assured us Huck would be cleared; the search was a routine formality. They were concerned about helping him cope with his double-barreled ordeal of losing his wife and being insulted by police intrusion.

An article about my experiences with Dana's case and the Long Beach Police Department was published in a local newspaper called *Beachcomber* in May 2018. The article *Accident or Unsolved Murder?* was written by Stephen Downing, a retired police officer. One of Huck's neighbors told the paper's publisher that Huck was innocent; I was out to get him. Another of Huck's neighbors sent me a scolding e-mail message. She wrote:

> "Your former brother-in-law might have been a liar, a philanderer, a monumental horse's ass, or whatever, but that doesn't make him a murderer. And considering that you are energetically attempting to prove him one and publishing your theories on the Internet, it's not surprising he has changed his name several times.
>
> You are not an objective person, you are very much an advocate; and advocates push their version of events. You have an uphill battle here. As I pointed out to Mr. Downing, your sister's accidental death—and that is what the coroner ruled it—is a closed case, not a cold case, which might at some point be reopened by the police. Your sister's tragic death occurred over four years ago. There is no evidence in police storage which might be re-examined. If Dana was cremated, then her remains are not available for exhumation and reexamination. There is no evidence that your former brother-in-law struck his wife on the head. There are no neighbors' statements that they heard fighting or any sort of commotion which might indicate that someone was being attacked (e.g., screaming or other unusual noises).
>
> You have theories about blood evidence which you believe existed, but there is no way at this late date to

prove or disprove them. I assume the police examined the entire house very thoroughly the night they spent so many hours there. They certainly weren't inside all that time doing nothing constructive. They confiscated the video tapes your former brother-in-law had and reviewed them. Have you ever seen them? The police certainly wouldn't let you review them, so I can't believe you have. Yet, you state that your sister was never seen moving around the house after a certain hour the night before the paramedics were called. How could you know that? And assuming the police advised you of that, it doesn't prove anything specific regarding the events leading up to Dana's death."

My point is that Huck, like Beal, has many passionate, vocal defenders. Their defenses ring with virtue. They don't have anything against Dana, if they think of Dana at all. She's dead and therefore no longer relevant. Rather, they are defending the person they see as the true victim. They are defending what they see as rule of law.

I'd like to emphasize that no public agency or authority has ever given credence to my claim Dana was murdered, and the inquiry was botched. Long Beach police found no evidence of a crime, and no evidence of investigative cock-up. The Los Angeles County Coroner found no evidence of foul play. The California Department of Justice found no credible allegation of criminal misconduct by officers. Prestigious lawyers have heard what I have to say and told me nothing can be done to bring a criminal complaint.

People in a position to do something about Dana's case are content to remain silent. City officials in Long Beach, for example, are aware of Dana's case. I say this because several computers using one static-IP address registered to the City of Long Beach have accessed the YogaDeath.com website more than 150 times over the course of a year.

In an email exchange in March 2019, Long Beach City Councilwoman Suzie Price wrote to me:

> "I am so sorry about your sister's loss. I can only imagine how you must feel with the incident being unresolved. It must feel like there is no justice. I am so sorry for that."

Price's note is the only communication I have received from a current public official acknowledging that something about Dana's case is unresolved. I thank Price for it.

Champions of the rule of law should rejoice that one grieving sister can't bend the system. But this shouldn't surprise anyone. The system wasn't made to serve grieving sisters or dead women. There's no such thing as a crime against a dead woman. Murder is a crime against "the people," as represented by institutions of state authority such as police, coroners, and prosecutors. If "the people" perceive no offense, is there a crime? No, at least not in the sense that the criminal justice system can do anything about it.

One of the hardest facts about Dana's case is that it's not unusual. It's an example of how the justice system works in Los Angeles County. It's an illustration of how Long Beach police kill complaints, bury misconduct, and avoid political consequences. This quote explains it well:

> "Government officials had one highly specific and tangible motive for supporting the local police; they wished to avoid liability in case of civil suits for damages. Burying or somehow justifying disagreeable episodes that might be costly in money and prestige would have to be given priority over any sense of moral responsibility. Consequently, at each level of government, the normal practice was collusion. Informal complaints were ignored, thereby never giving them an effective existence. Complainants were referred from office to office until they wearied. Officials at all levels of government united to obstruct or repel formal complaints."

The quote is from *Brutal Justice: The Ordeal of an American City* by Henry Cohen, an exposé of misconduct in the Long Beach Police Department published in 1980. Cohen's analysis was apt 40 years ago, and it's apt today. Cohen pointed out that only a small percentage of officers engaged in misconduct, but it was enough to corrode the department and drive honest officers out of the force.

I think about all the officers working on Dana's case, talking to neighbors and filing prompt, informative reports. I imagine it would be disheartening to learn that the lead detective disregarded what they wrote, bungled the case, and was protected by his superiors.

The handling of Dana's case up the chain of command was and is business as usual in Long Beach. The situation is beyond any good-faith resolution. What's left for me to do, then, other than tell the story?

In 2014, I posted a memorial website for Dana online. When I obtained the audio from Huck's 911 call, I posted it on the site. When I found out Huck had changed his name again, I included his various names and some biographical details on the site. He was participating in online message boards for widows and widowers, I learned. I wanted the women he wooed with his pitiable tale of personal tragedy to be able to fact-check him. If a woman searched online for him under any of the names of his that I knew, she would find Dana's site.

Marian, who had since sold her house in Long Beach and moved to Arkansas, found Dana's site and posted this comment in 2015:

> "there is so much more to the story than stated above. I knew them both well as I was their neighbor and acupuncturist. Hucky treated Dana like a queen she wanted for nothing he provided her with love, a beautiful home, made all three meals, including home made almond milk he made for her, he cleaned the house almost daily took care of the extensive gardens and pond and catered to her every need. ,He ran errands for Dana and did so much more. Dana and I talked frequently and she usually talked about how wonderful and kind huck was to her, she felt safe and loved and told me she loved being married to Huck. She loved that he was able to stay home and be with

her and their dog Enzo which he walked several times a day (Enzo is hyper and needed this) Hucky is devastated with his loss he will always love dana and she truly loved him If dana was here she would be horrified with what has been said and written about her love hucky please don't believe these hurtful cruel statements above there is so much left out. there were written by someone who does not even live in California . I hope you can rest in peace Dana Love Marian"

Marian painted a rosy picture of Dana's marriage that, unfortunately, did not accord with reality. It strikes me as a statement of wishful longing as much as a defense of Huck. Perhaps Marian dreamed of having this type of relationship with him.

On a website called Second Firsts, I found a "Letter to Heaven" that Huck had written, addressed to Dana. Huck wrote:

"...I never cried when my Mom died and I never cried when my Dad died and I never cried during our 14 years of marriage and now my tears flow daily, my tears hurt as they are like acid. I was supposed to die first not you! You have family here on earth I do not. Your family who for 14 years I thought were my family has abandoned me, now I'm left processing my anger towards them and trying not to let it destroy me. It's made me see why you chose to live so far from them, they will never be as true as you were...."

For the record, yes, I do see an implicit threat in Huck's expression of destructive anger toward my family. Yes, I do think he is serious and capable of acting on this threat. Yes, this threat does frighten me. However, I doubt the state is offended on my behalf. As a spokesperson for state authority might say: "No public health hazard to family or community is suspected or discovered."

The death of Christine Beal is another case in which the state saw no offense. Ten years prior to the bombing that killed Stephen Beal's ex-girlfriend, the death of Beal's wife Christine became a coroner's case. A coroner investigator wrote regarding the woman, who was dead in Long Beach at the age of 48:

> "Her medical history was unknown, with decedent's husband reported as uncooperative, not wanting to 'reveal' information to the hospital staff about the decedent. …Additional medical history included a recent fall down a flight of stairs on 02/16/08, as decedent and her husband attempted to move a piece of furniture; the bureau had fallen on her pelvic and hip area."

Medical examiner Eugene Carpenter, Jr., M.D., noted that Christine Beal suffered from chronic lead poisoning, too. He wrote:

> "Death is from pancreatitis, other known factors and other unknown factors. The findings are not sufficient to understand the cause(s) of death. Whether or not trauma played any role is not known. There is no evidence of foul play. Death is probably natural, maybe trauma contributed but this is not known. No public health hazard to family or community is suspected or discovered."

Christine Beal's manner of death remained undetermined. No further investigation was pursued. Reportedly, Long Beach police were not even notified about her case. I have little confidence that, if Long Beach police had investigated at the time, they would've found foul play. Only in retrospect, after the bombing, did authorities turn a critical eye on the case. I wonder how many deaths by dubious accident or "other unknown factors" in Los Angeles County may one day seem like foreshadowing of dark cases to come.

One bit of good news is that Long Beach police eventually removed Detective Todd Johnson from the homicide squad. A police spokeswoman confirmed this in April 2019 but did not say why or when it happened. Johnson is still on the force, reportedly. I've heard he's assigned to domestic violence cases, but the department hasn't confirmed this.

As time passes, I give less and less thought to Huck. When I look at family photos, it's jarring sometimes to see his toothy leer next to Dana's happy smile. But usually, he doesn't register. I know he's out there, lurking like an undiagnosed malignancy. Other matters of life and death are more immediate to me now, and I don't have the wherewithal to worry about him.

On the night of the Academy Awards in 2019, my brother Stephen and I talked about how we associated the night with Dana. Five years earlier, she was alive; on Monday after the Oscars, she was brain-dead in a hospital.

On Monday after the Oscars in 2019, Stephen called me in distress. He was driving when he lost control of his right arm and leg. He managed to pull into a parking lot. I picked him up and rushed him to a hospital. Was it a stroke or a seizure? Doctors ran tests and discovered a fast-growing brain tumor, a terminal one called a glioblastoma. Doctors don't know what caused it. Unscientifically, I wonder whether the unresolved trauma of Dana's case might have contributed. But that's just me; he doesn't blame the police.

Dana continues to be present in my thoughts, as she always has been in my life, even when we lived on opposite coasts. I wish I could see her, but I don't feel as if she's gone. In fact, I get the feeling she's fine. I get the feeling she doesn't blame the police, either. It's more like she's sad they let themselves down.

ABOUT THE AUTHOR

Lisa Jones is a web developer and LEVA-certified forensic video technician in Denver, Colorado.